FRATTON

LOCOMOTIVE DEPOT

A BRIEF HISTORY (1891-1967)

MICHAEL G. HARVEY

An early 1950s picture of Fratton depot allocated class "E1" 0-6-0 tank No. 32139 it is seen resting between its duties in the depot yard. This William Stroudley designed locomotive was introduced in 1874, No. 32139 lasted until 1958. During the 1950s, its classmate No. 32138 along with Fratton allocated class "02" 0-4-4 tank No. 30207 found regular employment on the twice daily goods between Fratton sidings and Portsmouth Royal Naval Dockyard. This duty entailed working "wrong line" up the 1 in 61 gradient to Portsmouth and Southsea (High Level) station to enable the train to entry into the Dockyard. In its heyday, the Dockyard railway system had over 30 miles of standard gauge track.
Photograph by the late Eric Grace.

Railway drivers and firemen based at Fratton locomotive depot worked local duties such as to Fareham and Gosport (west of Portsmouth) and to Havant and Chichester (east of Portsmouth) together with other stations. This 1947 photograph depicts a Class "L" 4-4-0 No. 31773, introduced in 1914, to a Wainwright SECR design - it is reversing into platform two, which today has now been buffered at a point near the rear of the "L"s tender. On the right can just be seen part of the tender of a Bulleid "pacific" en route with a train from Exeter Central to Brighton via Southampton Central, Cosham and Chichester. On the far left is platform three, this platform being used for trains from Portsmouth and Gosport travelling via Botley, the latter being where a branch line went to Bishops Waltham (Meon Valley Line). Class "L" 4-4-0s had large driving wheels of 6'8" diameter. *The late Denis Callender.*

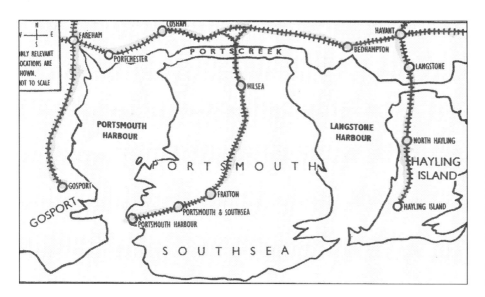

PORTSMOUTH, as can be seen, is an island, separated from the mainland by a narrow strip of water known as Portscreek. The branch line from Fareham to Gosport was opened in 1841 and then to Portsmouth in 1847 - the branch line from Havant to Hayling Island opened in 1867 and closed in 1963.

Front cover: Urie designed class "S15" 4-6-0 No. 30506 (allocated to Feltham depot 70B) awaits its next duty in Fratton yard. This is a 1958 picture, note the complete roundhouse roof, over the ensuing years this roof gradually deteriorated. No. 30506 has been preserved, and can be seen today at the Mid Hants Railway "Watercress Line". *From an original oil painting by Graham Beech.*

Back cover photograph: A late 1950s photograph of North Hayling station, an unusual one, has an abundance of passengers awaiting to board the train to Hayling Island! Normally at this halt only one or two passengers were the norm – there must have been a special party on this occasion. *N. E. Stead*

ISBN 9780957336742
First published 2012 by Tricorn Books. Republished 2014 by Kingfisher Productions. Printed and bound in the UK.
Design © 131 Design Ltd www.131design.org. Text & Images © Michael Harvey. Michael Harvey has asserted his right under the Copyright, Design and Patents Act 1988 to be identified as the author of this work. This book is sold subject to the conditions that it shall not by way of trade or otherwise, be lent, resold, hired out or otherwise circulated without the publisher's prior consent in any form of binding or cover other than that in which it is published and without a similar condition including this condition being imposed on the subsequent purchaser. Kingfisher Productions, www.railwayvideo.com

CONTENTS

The water tower at Fratton was a massive structure, but it also had other uses, as will be revealed later!
Brian Moss

FREIGHT LOCOMOTIVE AT FRATTON DEPOT . . .

It was quite rare to see a Bulleid designed class "Q1" 0-6-0 in a clean condition - this one, No. 33020, allocated to Eastleigh depot (71A) had just recently emerged from overhaul at Eastleigh Works, hence its pristine condition.

The late Eric Grace.

PASSENGER LOCOMOTIVE AT FRATTON STATION . . .

Class "N15" 4-6-0 No. 30753 *Melisande* departs from platform 2 with a passenger train terminating at Portsmouth and Southsea (Low Level).

Photograph by the late Eric Grace.

FOREWORD

This book deals primarily with a brief history of the running shed at Fratton, highlighting its steam locomotive drivers, firemen, cleaners, depot staff, crane operators, carriage and wagon inspectors, station staff and numerous other posts.

I have not included too much historical background of the more distant areas that Fratton depot locomotives frequented, as this book leans basically towards its local workings and a band of men that breathed steam, and lived their lives with the effects of sweat, dust and grime, in conditions that would certainly not be tolerated in today's world. The majority of the photographs that follow were taken by the late Eric Grace with his trusty Pentax camera, mostly relating to the mid 1950s up to the demise of SR steam in 1967. I am most grateful to Ann Grace, widow of Eric, for allowing the use of Eric's wonderful photographs.

Eric Grace had the foresight, even all those years ago, of capturing the unusual situations, such as groups and single portraits of his own fellow workers, going about their respective tasks, oblivious to the presence of the lurking camera man.

There were also many other camera happy chaps that worked Fratton depot and other local locations. Also, we should not forget those teenagers pursuing their hobby of train-spotting always at the ready to capture a black and white photograph in the shed round-house or yard - that is if they had mastered the art of eluding the dreaded shed foreman, Mr. Butler!

All pictures have been credited, and include some of my friends, together with a sprinkling of my own collection published in my "Diary of a Train-spotter" books. To recap ... those shots by Eric Grace will no doubt bring back numerous long gone memories to the readers in the heyday of British Railways steam - such marvellous memories that have been preserved in print for future generations to savour.

I must thank Eddie Rooke, as co-author of our book "Railway Heritage (Portsmouth)" - published by Silver Link in 1997, for his excellent descriptions of locations relating to local railways, and his knowledge of the subject, some of which relate to this book.

INTRODUCTION

When you read about Fratton locomotive depot it will no doubt provide evidence of its definitive history not only for those who were employed there but also for the teenage railway enthusiasts who's hobby was train-spotting. Those days of steam, grime and dust that were the norm every day hazard that drivers, firemen and many others had to endure, was a part of their life ... these men breathed steam! They received their wages for doing a job that they enjoyed, even though it virtually drained every ounce of energy and sweat from their bodies.

My passion for steam locomotives on the BR system, especially the period relating to the 1950s and 1960s has always been apparent, this being obvious by the fact that my previously published railway books.

I, and many of my teenage railway mates grew up in the shadow of Fratton depot and the station footbridge, when our hobby of train-spotting was in its heyday. As many already know, Fratton depot proved to be the most difficult to "bunk" as we always seemed to meet Mr. Butler the foreman, he just appeared from nowhere to "nab" us, we really should have had official permits!

Portsmouth is Britain's only island city, a fact that many people living away from this city are unaware of, this being by virtue of a narrow channel of water known as Portscreek which isolates it from the mainland.

The original name for Portsmouth was Portsea Island with its boundary within the island, not like today where its area has spread onto the mainland. The city is roughly 5 and a half miles north to south and three-and-half miles from west to east, and its population stands at around 250,000 this includes its boundaries. In fact, the city has the distinction of being Britain's most densely populated, as any car driver will no doubt let you know! It has been a pleasure getting involved with ex-Fratton depot workers and collecting their numerous memories. Many of these men will reunite long gone incidents both serious and amusing - bringing them back to life via the publication of this book. Their names will be in print for future generations to savour and remind them what the working conditions were really like during the heyday of steam-hauled trains on BR.

Michael G. Harvey.

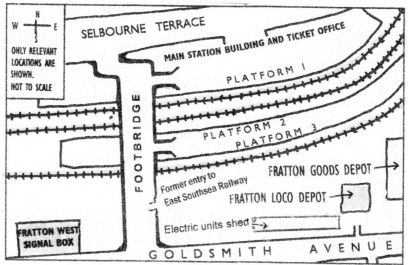

Fratton station area and road leading to the locomotive depot. To aid clarity some railway tracks have been omitted. Fratton East signal box, in relation to the West signal box, shown on this map, is in the north east curve area.

 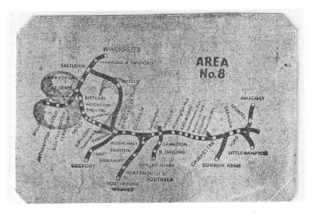

This is a Holiday Run-about Ticket that Eric Grace was issued in 1951. Eric, and a friend, usually travelled to the areas shown on the map to take photographs of the steam locomotives. Note: at that date, being a railwayman, he paid half fare, which was 6 shillings and 3d, for its seven day use.

The late Eric Grace, Fratton depot fireman and then driver, in the days of steam hauled trains. His fireman took the picture of Eric in the cab of class "N" No. 31411 on the north side of the Cosham triangle in 1963.

CHAPTER I

THE FIRST STEAM TRAIN INTO PORTSMOUTH

It was on Saturday 14 June 1847 that the citizens of Portsmouth saw its very first train arrive at Portsmouth Town station . . . and it was not without some problems. It originated from London (Victoria) via Chichester and Havant on the LBSCR route, but it came to grief as it departed from Fratton station, the tall chimney of the steam locomotive got jammed under Fratton Road bridge!

Railway workers from Fratton depot were hastily summoned, armed with pick axes and shovels to dig away ballast from beneath the locomotive's wheels, just enough space for the locomotive to continue its journey!

Needless to say, this embarrassed the Railway Company. What should have been a joyful occasion turned out to be just the opposite - a scant report of the trains' arrival was made in the local newspaper.

As there were no such facilities as loud speakers or information screens in those days, it was the duty of the station master to get his staff to assist by announcing details to passengers of the late arrival, this being via loud hailers . . . this must have caused a certain amount of embarrassment when the message went something like "Sorry for delay, this being due to the tall steam engines' chimney getting jammed under Fratton Bridge!"

Whatever reasons are given for the lateness of trains in today's modern system, none could compare with the one described - the incident was published in the local newspaper "The Hampshire Telegraph and Post" on 18 June 1847. Details regarding the incident were kept at a low profile, in fact, this newspaper was allotted one very short single column of print, this being virtually lost to its readers.

This was hardly the way to promote the coming of the railway to the City of Portsmouth!

Whilst mentioning Portsmouth Town railway station, this title was given to it until 1921, when it then became known as Portsmouth and Southsea. Most Portmuthians seemed to prefer its original name and even today many of its senior citizens still refer to it as the "Town" station. Even todays modern road signs include the word "Town."

"FLY TO THE FERRY, MADAM"?

Following the somewhat amusing antics relating to the first train to arrive in Portsmouth, local, "Portmuthians" were certainly not amused, bearing in mind that Gosport had its railway six years prior to Portsmouth, in 1841. Those passengers travelling to Portsmouth from London before 1847 needed to make the considerable walk from the station to catch the ferry to Portsmouth. The ferry being open to all the elements did not encourage those to travel! To enable passengers with heavy luggage to make their way to the ferry, a crude form of transport was available, this being hand drawn carts with luggage and seating space known as 'Flys'. A small charge was made for this facility; you could say that this was the forerunner of the taxi.

CHAPTER 2

SOME EARLY GWR OBSERVATIONS

Basil Batten

Just over 250 Collett designed class 4900 (Hall) 4-6-0s were introduced in 1928 primarily for mixed traffic use.

A "Modified" version designed by Hawkesworth were introduced in 1944 - a total of 71 were built.

The late Basil Batten had the distinction of noting some of the very first Great Western Region steam locomotives that found their way into Portsmouth in the period between 1900 up to the late 1920s. He resided at a location close to Fratton station, an ideal vantage point. In latter years, the early 1960s, he moved to a similar view point, at the western end of the Cosham triangle.

My earliest memories relating to Great Western Region steam was during the early 1930's in those days the "Star" and the "Saint" 4-6-0s were regular visitors. The 4 cylinder "Star" class included No. 4027 *Norwegian Monarch,* others were Nos 4001 *Dog Star,* 4034 *Queen Adelaide,* 4058 *Princess Augusta,* and No. 4068 *Llanthony Abbey,* the latter having been withdrawn in 1938, had parts utilised in "Castle" class No. 5088 which was also named *Llanthony Abbey.*

The very first football excursions into Portsmouth, were terminated at platform three at Fratton, were from the Birmingham area and were 'Hall' class Nos. 4949 *Packwood Hall* and 4947 *Nanhoran Hall* - in the early 1930s.

Other such GWR engines also made inroads to Portsmouth, such as No. 3323 *Etona,* a "Bulldog" class, this being in August 1930 employed on a train from Reading General to Portsmouth and Southsea Low Level.

The "Saint" class 4-6-0s had some magical names, those I recall were Nos. 2909 *Lady of Provence,* 2918 *Saint Catherine,* 2926 *Saint Nicholas,* 2930 *Saint Vincent,* 2978 *Kirkland* and 2980 *Coeur de Lion* - introduced in 1902.

Class "4900" (Hall) 4-6-0 locomotive No. 4902 *Aldenham Hall* in a cloud of steam, as it enters platform one at Fratton station with a Portsmouth and Southsea (Low Level) to Reading General train in the late 1950s.
Derek Spicer

CHAPTER 3

FRATTON DEPOT: DIESEL-FREE

In its lifetime Fratton depot had the distinction of not ever having any BR diesel locomotives in its allocation, although when being constructed between 1889 and 1891, it was thought that a "Service" diesel mechanical assisted in the construction of the building.   From the early 1950s up to its final demise in 1967, 0-6-0 diesel shunters from Eastleigh (71A) were to be seen in the yard and shunting in the Field sidings. Also, quite surprising, was that no Standard class locomotives were shedded at Fratton - although numerous class "4" 2-6-0s, class "4" 4-6-0s and class "5" 4-6-0s were a common sight in and around the Fratton area. I recall certain Standard class engines that seemed to always be seen in Portsmouth - those that fall into this category were class "4" 2-6-0s Nos. 76005, 76008, 76015, 76017, 76060, 76066, 76067 and 76069. No. 76017 is today in preservation at the Mid Hants Railway, awaiting overhaul. Class "4" 2-6-4 tanks were also frequent visitors.

In 1958 Fratton locomotive depot was classed as 70F in the Southern Region 70s list. The complete codes under this heading were as follows:

70A NINE ELMS; 70B FELTHAM; 70C GUILDFORD; 70D BASINGSTOKE; 70E READING (South); 70F FRATTON; 70G NEWPORT (Isle of Wight); and 70H RYDE (Isle of Wight).

Shed plates were carried by all BR steam locomotives, these being in the form of an oval disc measuring about 7" across and 5" from top to bottom. These plates being fixed in the lower central half of the locomotives' smoke box door, uniform colours were white for code with a black background.   Coloured number plates on some Standard classes were made of wood, with numerals made from soup cans by Eastleigh fitter Ron Cover, late 1966 to 1967. This practice was also displayed by colouring numbers of the smoke box door locomotives' number.

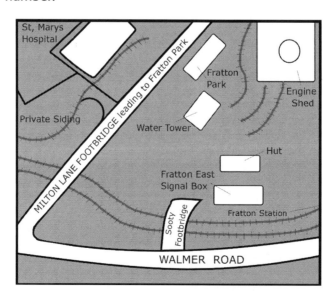

A map showing locations of "Sooty" footbridge and Fratton depot and yard. To aid clarity, some lines have been omitted.

CHAPTER 4

AN ENGINE SHED IS BORN

The engine shed at Fratton was built in the period 1889 to 1891 as a JOINT venture between the LBSCR (London Brighton and South West Railway) and the LSWR (London and South Western Railway) and in this respect was rare. Fratton was one of two sheds that was shared by separate companies - the other being Aberdeen (Ferryhill), which was shared by the Caledonian and North British companies.

It had been suggested, probably incorrectly, that the site of an earlier and smaller shed at Fratton was erected on the site of a smaller shed that dated back to the 1860s, but this is not confirmed. What is certain, was that a smaller four lane shed, built by the LBSCR before the 1850s or earlier, this being sited east of Blackfriars Road footbridge - on the north side of the main lines close to the Town station.

It was an obvious plan to erect engine sheds close to stations they served, and equally it was not unusual for the Portsmouth area to become congested as over the years railway activity expanded.

With the passage of time increased traffic dictated larger facilities, and from this situation, it was necessary to site the replacement on an ideal open space some distance from the station. This then involved the "dead mileage" of engines having to run "light" both to and from the engine shed.

An 1859 diagram of the Town station depicts the LBSCR shed on the south side of the main lines at the eastern end of the goods yard and west of the substantial sized footbridge, locally known as "Jacobs Ladder", It was here that a turntable with four sidings leading off was situated along with also a fifth quite short siding being evident. This would seem to have been an engine handling and parking area for the use of one of the two railway companies, presumably the LSWR?

A general view of Fratton locomotive yard taken from the east signal box area. Several Standard class locomotives and the coaling crane (DS200) are prominent. Today this area has been completely obliterated and has been replaced by the "Pompey Centre" consisting of new roads, industrial units, a new entrance to Fratton Park and the largest B&Q warehouse in Great Britain. This is an April 1963 picture. *Photograph by the late Eric Grace.*

Boundaries changed at a later date, and the site of the turn-table was omitted, it had now been covered by the extension of Greetham Street, being outside of the new perimeter.

As Fratton locomotive depot came into use, its predecessor at the Town station was then demolished, leaving the site in use for servicing engines between their duties, with stabling and water facilities and a 50 foot turn-table together with a brick built "signing on" hut.

This situation virtually remained the same until the demise of SR steam in July 1967. Larger main-line engines unable to use the turn-table, had always then to return to Fratton depot. The building was designed on the roundhouse principle with a central turn-table that was 50 foot in diameter from which radiated 24 stabling roads (one was removed later).

The bickering between the LBSCR and the LSWR continued - as HALF were owned by the two companies, and the division that extended out into the shed yard was very scrupulously respected by their staffs. Indeed, it had been reported that the two companies' employees acted as though they were oblivious of the others existence!

At its height, probably in the early and mid 1930s, and successive years, its allocation of steam locomotives stood at the staggering number of 70. The most common being the Drummond designed class "T9" 4-4-0 mainline passenger engines that were built in 1899 and 1900 - they were known by their drivers and firemen as "Greyhounds" relating to their speedy running.

The sole named passenger engines ever allocated to Fratton were a batch of ten class "V" - more commonly known as the "Schools" class. These ten allocations were primarily for the working of the Portsmouth Harbour to London (Waterloo)

"Schools" class 4-4-0 No 30905 *Tonbridge* departs from Fratton station (platform two) with a train from Basingstoke via Winchester and Fareham. Ten of this class were allocated to Fratton depot prior to the third rail electrification in 1937 they were primarily used on the Portsmouth Harbour to Waterloo "Direct Line" passenger services.   *Michael G. Harvey*

No. 30924 *Haileybury*	No. 30929 *Malvern*	
No. 30925 *Cheltenham*	No. 30930 *Radley*	
No. 30926 *Repton*	No. 30931 *King's Wimbledon*	
No. 30927 *Clifton*	No. 30932 *Blundells*	The ten "Schools" include all the three
No. 30928 *Stowe*	No. 30933 *King's Canterbury*	that are in preservation today, these being Nos. 30925, 30926 and 30928.

direct route via Havant and Guildford. But with the coming of the third rail electrification on this route in 1937, the "Schools" were not required and, subsequently re-allocated elsewhere, such as Nine Elms (70A), Stewarts Lane (73A) and Bricklayers Arms (73B).

Of the ten "Schools" allocated to Fratton, it was known that six were employed on the Portsmouth to Waterloo "Direct Line" workings, (ex-drivers have confirmed this), and sometimes, during busy days an additional locomotive was in use on anyone day of the week.

These powerful locomotives, designed by R. E. L. Maunsell, had the distinction of being the most powerful 4-4-0 wheel arrangement in Europe. The first 20 out of a class of 40 were all built between March 1930 and August 1935. Their number series being 30900 to 30939.

The final steam-hauled workings on the "Direct Line" of which the "Schools" were ideally suited, took place on Saturday 3 July 1937 - this being the 9.50pm from Waterloo and the 9.30pm from Portsmouth and Southsea (Low Level), both steam-hauled trains arrived at their destinations in the very early minutes of Sunday morning.

It was one of these 4-4-0s that worked the final steam to the Harbour station, No. 931 *Kings Wimbledon* had hauled the 3.30pm "down" train. The 9.30 am to Waterloo was a Nine Elms (70A) duty No. 2, together with the 4.50pm to Portsmouth they were often in the hands of either a "King Arthur" 4-6-0 or a "Remembrance" 4-6-0.

Fratton had its pump house next to the roundhouse - this catered for 14 converted coal-fired locomotives to oil-fired, as at 3 July 1948 - but by this date many of those locomotives were lying redundant in the sidings at Fratton.

Some of the older types, such as No. 206, a class "B2X" 4-6-0 was used as an oil-burner, even though it was introduced as far back as 1897 it was proved to be un-successful. "West Country" and "King Arthur" class engines were converted to oil burners, but with little success.

The reason for going back to coal-fire was that the coal shortage was over, and oil was more expensive because it was imported.

Prominent classes at this date were "A1X" tanks, "M7" tanks, "T9" 4-4-0s and "C2X" 0-6-0s. As at 3 July 1948 a few oil-fired engines were converted back to coal-fired this included class "U" 2-6-0 No. 31625 - it can be seen on the Mid Hants Railway today, but it is "Out of Use."

Fratton depot (71D) summer 1948

30027	30045	30054	30113	30114
30115	30118	30280	30287	30303
30305	30314	30338	30400	30401
30402	30404	30415	30417	30480
30731	31625	31831	32153	32490
32492	32509	32537	32548	32554
32559	32644	32655	32659	32662

A brace of oil-burning 4-4-0s stored in Fratton goods siding awaiting to be towed to Eastleigh Works for scrapping.
The late Eric Grace.

CHAPTER 5

GRADUAL ELIMINATION OF STEAM

Portsmouth city boundaries extend quite some way to the east and west of the former Farlington Halt and Paulsgrove Halt respectively both now extinct - so trains routed across the northern side of the Cosham triangle are regarded as having worked "through Portsmouth" without even penetrating the main part of the city on Portsea Island.

The elimination of haulage by the steam locomotive on British Railways was a protracted process from which arose two main causes - mostly from the closure of routes and services, and from alternative forms of transport, and in almost every case this being diesel or electric power.

Except where a route was shut down completely, substitution for steam by alternative traction often affected just passenger traffic only - and freight trains conveying parcels and other items, as well as long distance through trains continued with steam haulage. Amongst these would be "Specials" such as the royal and VIP trains, day excursions, rail tours etc, these continued, in some cases, for decades, to be steam-hauled over that route.

In the Portsmouth area, routes closed included the Cosham to Havant "shuttle" (this ran from a single line branching off the "up" platform, adjacent to the rear of houses in Windsor Road) - it was in one of those houses that the author Michael Harvey lived in between 1970 and 1978.

Also succumbed to closure were in later years the East Southsea branch (see page 23), the local Lee-on-the-Solent and the Gosport branches together with those on the Meon Valley between Fareham and Alton and, not forgetting those to the Royal Naval Dockyard and the much-loved Hayling Island branch.

In terms of numbers of Fratton allocated steam locomotives, none of these was particularly significant, although they did cover some quite interesting types.

On the other hand, the two Portsmouth electrification schemes of 1937 and 1938 constituted some major steps in helping to reduce steam haulage in the area.

They brought third rail operation by electric multiple units (EMU) to much of the triangle between London, Brighton and Portsmouth - plus Woking to Guildford and Alton, where it had already been introduced.

Under the nationalisation of British Railways in 1948, not too many years elapsed before a decision was taken to commence total elimination of steam motive power in favour of, primarily full scale dieselisation together with some measure of electrification.

Destruction of thousands of steam engines including many of those built as recently as 1951, were, in a word "scrapped" — these included class "9F" 2-10-0 freight types and the "Britannia" class main-line "pacific" passenger locomotives.

They had less than ten or fifteen years service before being sent to the scrap yards.

The 1957 "Hampshire" diesel units scheme involved the operation of local passenger services in the Hampshire area and just into Wiltshire and Berkshire. Lines affected were Southampton Terminus-Alton, Portsmouth-Southampton Salisbury. Portsmouth-Eastleigh, Romsey-Andover Junction and subsequently Southampton Terminus to Reading by diesel multiple units.

The former Pump House   *Michael G. Harvey*

Fratton depot was virtually unique in that it was the sole complete roundhouse designed example on the Southern Region. There were semi round houses on the the SR at both Guildford (70C) and Horsham (75D), the latter were quite rare as only St Blazey (83E) in Cornwall and one other in the north East of England were the only known types.

Having said that Fratton was the only complete roundhouse on the SR, it has been brought to light that Eastbourne also had one. Apparently, there existed a complete roundhouse at New Cross Gate and a total of three enclosed structures at Battersea Park - both were LBSCR structures and still stand today in alternative commercial use.

By the mid 1960s, and no longer in use as a running shed, Fratton roundhouse found that there was ample space, albeit the roofing had seen better days, in which they could "store" surplus steam locomotives pending possible preservation, and in relative safeness, together with a degree of cover and protection.

The foreman had by this date given up his evicting of us local train-spotters, I even recall a visit in 1964 when the well known club secretary of a North London group an old friend of mine, Ernie Middleton, brought a 25 seater coach of enthusiasts to Fratton, without any official permit. A very similar situation I had with Ernie was back in 1958 when a coach full of trainspotters attempted to "bunk" Grantham depot - on that occasion Ernie was asked for his permit - "I do not have one" he replied - Ernie was heard to say "there are 25 of us and only one foreman" Ernie urged us to complete the visit at gross speed.

Portsmouth train spotters, unsuccessfully tried to obtain surplus items from redundant steam engines, to keep as souvenirs, but it was revealed, some years later, that one of my and Eddie Rooke's mates somehow managed to remove a name-plate from a redundant locomotive and took it home for safe keeping, but the person in question got somewhat nervous of his acquisition, and decided to dispose of it by taking it during the night - and dumping it in the bed of the former Arundel and Portsmouth Canal at Eastney. Whether the story is true is debatable, but if, in coming years this site was to be cleared, the truth would then be revealed! It would certainly sell to modern day enthusiasts for their collection.

Going back to the "stored" engines this was not the first time that Fratton depot was used for storage - as in 1948 a considerable batch of steam engines that had been converted to oil burning, in a bid to save coal after WW2 were stored in the Field sidings, adjacent to Fratton Park, home of Portsmouth Football Club (1898).

After the war, Fratton had its own pump house, adjoining the main depot, this provided the gas for re-fuelling oil- burning engines. The majority of oil-burners were eventually towed off to Eastleigh Works for scrap.

Mid 1960s was the time when preservation of certain classes of former BR steam were put aside for posterity to admire. It was thought that "Lord Nelson" class 4-6-0 No. 30850 *Lord Nelson,* would be a candidate as appropriately being Portsmouth, and Lord Nelson's HMS *Victory* was berthed in the dockyard. Others followed such as "King Arthur" class 4-6-0 No. 30777 *Sir Lamiel,* class "V" 4-4-0 No. 30925 *Cheltenham,* class "T9" 4-4-0 No. 30120, Class "M7" 0-4-4 tank No. 30245 and a Beattie well tank of class "0298"a 2-4-0 wheel arrangement, (this and a class "Z" heavy 0-8-0 tank No. 30952) had never been to Fratton before. But, unfortunately, the "Z" was cut up at Eastleigh Works, the Bluebell Steam Railway were hoping to purchase it, but at that time, funds were insufficient enough to obtain the locomotive.

Others also came to be stored, this included a class "L1" 4-4-0 No. 31757, a victim of the Kent area electrification scheme, it remained with a tarpaulin over its chimney for a considerable time before being towed to Eastleigh for scrap.

Another tank engine, a class "M7" 0-4-4 No. 30133 was hoped to be set aside for possible preservation, not for its own sake but as a source as a boiler for a Peter Drummond designed locomotive this being a Highland Railway 4-4-0 No. 54398 *Ben Alder* of the Scottish Region. Sadly, this interesting project floundered, and "M7" No. 30133 was later cut up for scrap.

During 1964 and 1965 a great amount of "stored" locomotives, those probably not being saved, were towed away from the depot and sidings by class "33" diesels to the yard at Salisbury depot (72B) to be prepared for towing to the scrap yard in South Wales. They left Fratton usually in batches of two or three at a time, it was recorded that on 13 September 1964 saw the beginning of this exodus, and many more found their way to the scrap yards.

Here are just two of numerous movements of withdrawn steam locomotives noted passing through Cosham station en route to Salisbury depot yard: class "33" No. D6528 towing class "U" 2-6-0 No. No. 31807 and class "N" 2-6-0 No. 31829, class "33" No. D6545 with "N" 2-6-0s Nos. 31830 and 31832. It was soon to be the end of the steam locomotive in Portsmouth after three quarters of a century of importance and effort. With the passing of the locomotives and their facilities, that have been used from the outset, and were no more required, the complete area was left to the ravages of time.

It was March 1969 when the final remains were disposed of. There were some reliable reports of railwaymen putting their belongings in a safe place, as they walked out of the depot for the last time ... the location will be revealed in a later page of this book!

This Stroudley designed class "E1" 0-6-0 tank locomotive No. 32694 (allocated to Fratton depot (70F) and introduced in 1874, was a regular turn on the twice daily Monday to Friday mixed goods to the Royal Naval Dockyard. It ran from the sidings via Fratton East signal box (shown here) from the late 1950s up until early 1960. It was hoped that this vintage tank engine would be saved for preservation, but it was not to be, and was sent to Eastleigh Works for scrapping in January 1961.
The late Eric Grace.

CHAPTER 6

STEAM DUTIES OF LOCOMOTIVES: 1920s to 1930s

THE MAJORITY OF THE STEAM LOCOMOTIVE CLASSES
MENTIONED BELOW HAD ALREADY BEEN WITHDRAWN BEFORE
MY HOBBY OF TRAIN-SPOTTING HAD STARTED IN 1955

These were the types of steam locomotives that would be frequently
observed in Portsmouth and, consequently at Fratton depot.

FORMER LOCAL RAILWAY ENTHUSIAST ALF COFFIN OFTEN MADE
VISITS TO THE SIDINGS ADJACENT TO GOLDSMITH AVENUE
'WITH HIS "BROWNIE" BOX CAMERA.

What handsome designed steam locomotives could be seen during the 1920s and 1930s, with examples such as the L. B. Billinton class "J2" 4-6-2 designed tank and the class "B4" 4-4-0s. No. 54 *Empress*, introduced 1900, had the distinction of hauling Queen Victoria's funeral train between Fareham and London in February 1901.

Fratton depot had the much known and highly respected railway photographer, H. C. Casserley visiting the depot in the early 1920s - two of the steam classes he made references to were a class "0330" 0-6-0 saddle-tank No. 835 and a William Adams designed class "0415" 4-4-2 radial tank No. 481 the former being introduced in 1876 and the latter in 1883 which took over before the "Direct" route was electrified by the addition of a third rail.

The Billinton designed class "B2X" 4-4-0s were certainly pleasant to the eye, the class of 25 locomotives were used extensively on the Portsmouth Harbour to London (Victoria) passenger trains - this being prior to the batch of ten "Schools" class 4-4-0s which took over before the "Direct" route was electrified by the addition of a third rail.

Side tanks of the class "D1" 0-4-2 types (a Stroudley design) were used on the Cosham to Chichester Motor trains they were fitted for push-and-pull.

No 174, a Gladstone designed 0-4-2 was named FRATTON and was cut up for scrap in 1930.

Class "D15" 4-4-0s Drummond design. Used on Portsmouth to Salisbury turns.

Class "K10" 4-4-0s. Forty built in early 1900s. Secondary passenger and freight duties. Known as "Small Hoppers".

Class "L12" 4-4-0s. Introduced 1904. Drummond design. Secondary passenger duties.

Class "S11" 4-4-0s. Duties as "L12s". Introduced 1903.

Class "T1" 0-4-4 tanks. Introduced 1894. General shunting work and pilot turns. One of this class could always be seen at Portsmouth and Southsea station as a "Station Pilot" for many years during the period of the late 1890s to mid 1930s.

Class "A1" and "A1X" 0-6-0 tanks were basically for use on the Hayling Island branch. They also had duties on the Gosport branch, at Bedenham sidings.

FRATTON DEPOT IN THE EARLY 1920s

This is a William Adams designed class "0415" 4-4-2 tank locomotive No. 481. It is in Fratton depot roundhouse, May 1920. No. 481 was built in 1883 and withdrawn in 1942. An example of this class can be seen today on the Bluebell Steam Railway in Sussex.   *H. C. Casserley*

A rare photograph of a saddle-tank steam locomotive in Fratton depot yard. It was photographed on 4th June 1921. It is a Beyer Peacocok designed 0-8-0ST numbered 335. They were known as "Saddle-backs". No. 335 was built in 1876 and withdrawn in 1943.   *H. C. Casserley*

"J2" No. 2326, a - "pacific" tank - was a L.B. Billinton design, built in 1912 it was originally named *Bessborough*. It was withdrawn in 1951.   *The late Alf Coffin*

CAMERA ON FRATTON YARD AREA 1920s & 1930s

Sixty class "02" 0-4-4T locomotives were built at Nine Elms Works between 1889 and 1895. Their main claim to fame is the fact that 23 of them were used on the Isle of Wight right up until the end of steam. In the final years of steam at Portsmouth, fellow class member No. 30207 was employed for many years as a regular on the Dockyard Goods. No. 185 pictured here was withdrawn in 1940. *The late Alf Coffin*

Billinton designed class "B2X" 4-4-0 No. 206 in its penultimate year of service. Prior to rebuilding from class "B2" between 1907 and 1916, the whole of this class of 25 engines was used on the Portsmouth to London route. This particular engine was built in 1897 and withdrawn in 1933. In 1903 and 1904 it was used unsuccessfully in oil firing trials. *The late Alf Coffin.*

Under minor repair on the hoist at the Goldsmith Avenue entrance of Fratton locomotive depot is one of William Adams elegantly designed class "T3" 4-4-0s No 561. Picture taken in 1920. Twenty of this class were built at Nine Elms Works between 1892 and 1893 - they had 6 ft. 7 inch driving wheels, No. 561 was withdrawn early 1930 along with 16 other "T3s". Luckily, one of its class mates, No. 563 has been preserved, it resides today at the National Railway Museum at York. *H. C. Casserley.*

COMMON AND RARE STEAM CLASSES IN PORTSMOUTH

Anyone that worked at Fratton depot, Portsmouth railway stations, or were just railway enthusiasts, would tell you that certain classes of steam locomotives were very common - such as class "U" and "N" 2-6-0s, class "T9" 4-4-0s, class "M7" 0-4-4 tanks, class "A1X" 0-6-0 tanks, Standard class "4" 2-6-0s and Standard class "5" 4-6-0s - all these, and others, were everyday notings, but what about those classes that were not normally seen at Fratton?

During the years 1957 to 1967, local train-spotters might have found some unusual classes turning up in Portsmouth, which has led me to highlight just a few in this category that arrived with various specials, excursions etc. My own notings, coupled with those of the late Basil Batten and other reliable sources are shown below. Note: some of these locomotives used the north side of the Cosham triangle, thus bypassing Fratton, but that's not to say that the locomotive did not run "light" to Fratton for coal and water this would happen (for example) if an excursion ran from Bristol to Bognor.

GWR engines	4082 *Windsor Castle*	Pannier tanks	4672
	4086 *Built Castle*	" "	4689
	5050 *Earl of St. Germans*	" "	9710
	5067 *St. Fagans Castle*		
	7801 *Anthony Manor*		
	7817 *Garsington Manor*		

SR engines	30072 class "USA" 0-6-0T		31247 class "D1" 4-4-0
	30587 class "0298" 2-4-0WT		
	30850 *Lord Nelson* - class "LN" 4-6-0		31735 " " "
	30856 *Lord St. Vincent* " "		
	30862 *Lord Collingwood* " "		
	30952 class "Z" 0-8-0T		
	31753 class "L1" 4-4-0		31775 class "L" 4-4-0
	31757 " " "		DS600 class "A1" 0-6-0T
	31786 " " "		DS680 class " "
	35007 *Aberdeen Commonwealth* - class "MN" 4-6-2		
	35011 *General Steam Navigation* " " "		
	35022 *Holland-America Line* - " " "		
	35026 *Lamport & Holt Line* - " " "		

LMR engines	43088 class "4" 2-6-0		45046 class "5" 4-6-0
	44768 class "5" 4-6-0		45246 class " "
	44770 class " "		48408 class "8F" 2-8-0
	44909 class " "		

| ER engines | 61119 and 61200 both class "B1" 4-6-0s |

Class "7" 4-6-2s	70000 *Britannia*	70017 *Arrow*
	70002 *Geoffrey Chaucer*	70037 *Hereward the Wake*
	70004 *William Shakespeare*	70047 (un-named)

Class "9F" 2-10-0s	92004	Class "9F" 2-10-0s	92212
	92206		92220 *Evening Star*
	92211		92239

| Class "WD" | 90261 2-8-0; | Standard class "3" 2-6-2T | 82028 |
| | | Standard class "2" 2-6-2T | 84021 |

CHAPTER 7

A FEW VARIED DUTIES OF FRATTON ENGINES

MOST OF THE LIST THAT FOLLOWS RELATES TO FRATTON
ALLOCATED STEAM IN THE 1950s AND 1960s

There were three class "E4" 0-6-2 tanks Nos. 32479, 32495 an 32509 of Billinton design built in 1910. Their time was spent shunting in the Field Sidings and empty carriage workings between Portsmouth Harbour and Fratton sidings. Whenever shunting was being carried out, the prominent "zig-zag" roof of the goods depot always filled the background.

At this point (1957) I have made mention that the number of Fratton steam engines in its allocation was just under 30 – this had more than halved, compared to its 1937 total.

Before further mention of engine duties, I have included the route into the engine shed - from the Town or Harbour stations. I refer to the locomotives that hauled the in-coming carriages.

An important structure, adjacent to the goods sidings was this British Road Services Depot. This being for goods that came in or departed by rail, transferring to road haulage to local points.   *Michael G. Harvey*

The engines having ran "light" - and in reverse, via the line adjacent to the washing unit and alongside of the electric unit depot at Goldsmith Avenue. They then used the triangle of tracks that included the British Road Services brick-built offices, where a buffer stop necessitated the engine to then run "forward" - at this point, the buffer stop almost reaching Frogmore Road, leading to Fratton Park.

This triangle was constructed in the early 1930s to allow the passage of larger and more powerful steam locomotives to turn round.

The class "M7" 0-4-4 tanks performed such jobs as empty carriage workings, but they could also be seen working turns not usually carried out such as the 12.15pm four carriage section of the Brighton to Plymouth service (as far as Fareham). I recall that there were three "M7s" at Fratton, Nos. 30022, 30039 and 30357.

The Drummond designed class "T9" 4-4-0s were the favourites of many local trainspotters, also of the drivers and firemen.

Their 1899 vintage might suggest that they were "clapped out" by the 1950s, but they soldiered on until the early 1960s. Duties were widespread, local passenger trains to Southampton, Andover Junction trains via Romsey, the Gosport branch and the Meon Valley line. Engines were Nos. 30726, 30729 and 30732.

The "U" class "moguls" were probably the most common class seen in Portsmouth. Like the "T9s" they were called upon to perform duties such as the Salisbury trains. Used on Sunday Excursions to Bournemouth and Weymouth. Seen on pw trains on weekend rail works. Fratton "Us" were Nos. 31637, 31638, 31805, 31807, 31808 and 31809. No. 31638 has been preserved at the "Bluebell Steam Railway".

Billinton designed class "K" 2-6-0s were highly thought of by drivers at Fratton, and their elegant design gave them a handsome look. Worked on pick-up freights between Portsmouth and Littlehampton, taking in Bognor, Barnham and Havant sidings. Sometimes used on the 12.15pm to Fareham.

There were just two at Fratton, Nos. 32337 and 32349, both were kept in immaculate condition.

I can confirm that one particular job for one of these two took place on Sunday 4 January 1959 (as I, and others were there to witness it) - the drama unfolds. I, with four teenage train-spotters were travelling by train to visit engine sheds in London, we were on the "Direct Line" via Guildford to Waterloo in a ten coach electric unit train (five sets of two-coach units). The weather was dreadful and snow drifts were encountered just south of Rowlands Castle station!

Our train became stranded in deep snow. After a wait of about 30 minutes, in which time a steam engine from Fratton had been summoned, it arrived tender first to assist the electric units - it was Fratton class "K" 2-6-0 No. 32349. It coupled up to our train and travelled at a steady pace until it reached Guildford station, where the conditions were much more favourable. No. 32349 retreated to the depot (70C) for coal and water. Our electric units then continued to London.

The Stroudley designed 0-6-0 tanks of class "E1" were one of the oldest steam design, being introduced way back in 1874! Fratton had Nos. 32139 and 32694, the latter being active until late 1960. Their duties included Hilsea Gas Works sidings, the Gosport branch and the twice daily Dockyard goods. It was hoped that 32694 might be preserved, but was sent to Eastleigh to be cut up.

Class "C2X" 0-6-0s were ancient-looking freight engines. They covered the pick-up goods trains at station sidings along the east bound LBSCR main line to Brighton, they helped with empty carriage duties. I never did see a "C2X" on a passenger train. Nos. 32548, 32549 and 32550 were the depots' engines, No. 32548 sported "double domes" Introduced in 1908.

Class H2" 4-4-2 No. 32424 *Beachy Head* allocated to Brighton (75A) was a frequent visitor to Fratton in the 1950s.

The late Eric Grace.

"Terriers" or class "A1X" 0-6-0 diminutive tanks were one of the late Eric Grace's most loved Fratton based engines. They worked the Havant to Hayling Island branch, until its closure in November 1963.

This branch line was much photographed, but the majority of Eric's pictures were taken at the depot. At 1957 there were Nos. 32640, 32646, 32650, 32661 and 32677 at Fratton.

During the 1940s, Fratton supplied steam engines to shunt the goods yard at Portsmouth and Southsea station, many varied classes were used. Rarities such as class "0330" 0-6-0 saddle-tanks and Adams designed class "G6" 0-6-0 side tanks of 1894 vintage were used. The aforementioned saddle-tanks were known as "Saddle-backs".

CHAPTER 8

RAILWAYMEN'S MEMORIES IN THE DAYS OF STEAM

JOHN SCUTT

I was employed as a guard based in Portsmouth and one of my memories that I recall took place on a Sunday in early 1964. This particular day was set aside for steam locomotive trials on the single track leading into Portsmouth Royal Naval Dockyard.

TWO PULLMAN CARRIAGES

There were two Bulleid designed "pacifics" a class "West Country" and a "Battle of Britain" double-heading just two Pullman carriages into the Dockyard, it was said that these originated from Southampton Docks. The route taken was via Fratton station to Portsmouth and Southsea High Level, working the "wrong line" up the 1 in 61 gradient to gain entry via the branch which closely followed the contours of Victoria Park.

The two "pacifics" made at least two further return trips with the Pullman carriages, with one locomotive at the front and the other at the rear.

ROAD CROSSINGS

The line then negotiated crossings at Edinburgh Road, Alfred Road and finally Unicorn Gate, this entrance was next to the former platform which had a canopy, the platform was used in earlier days to pick up sailors going on "draft" - scars of the canopy can still be seen today. The guard on this train was former Fratton based railwayman Jimmy Stallard.

This "weight trial" was quite unusal as normally only small Fratton tank engines or sometimes class "U" or "N" 2-6-0s were seen on this branch.

NOTHING REPORTED

It appeared that there were no official reports relating to these most unusual workings in any railway journal or magazine, and the question of whether the outcome had any significance in later years must remain unanswered, as many of the local railwaymen involved are no longer with us.

The answer to that final question may have been, that in 2010, a single Freight-Liner siding was laid adjacent to the Fratton station to allow diesel-hauled goods to convey such items as bananas to the North West of England.

These having been unloaded from banana ships from Cyprus to the berthing docks in Portsmouth Harbour and taken by road (during the early hours) and then onto the waiting FL train.

FIRST GOODS FOR 27 YEARS

This new service, did not really get off the ground, as it lasted only for a short time. Anyway, the goods that were carried from this new terminal, was the first seen in Portsmouth for 27 years.

At the date of compilation of this book, I reside in Cosham.

My interest in railways still continues today, especially the steam-hauled "Specials" that pass by my window at Cosham station, but these are very infrequent - more than likely, they are diesel-hauled by a class "66" or a "47".

I recall that from 1935, my father worked for Chaplin's, which were agents for the Southern Railway, and delivered the majority of the goods that came into Portsmouth by rail - this location being the goods shed under Portsmouth and Southsea High Level platforms. This building was entered via a large pair of double gates directly opposite the imposing feature of the Guildhall. As a small lad, I often assisted my father at this location.

PLA FOR ONE SHILLING

Portsmouth's main station consisted of both a five platform Low Level and a two platform High Level layout. I have many fond memories of the busy summer months, which saw the station absolutely packed tight with "PLA" (Passengers Luggage in Advance) and this was basically luggage in the form of attache cases and parcels sent from ANY location on BR to Portsmouth in advance of the passenger - and, no matter what the distance, the cost for this facility was a fixed cost of just one shilling. The luggage was piled high, and even obliterated the station clock on some occasions - especially if it was a Bank holiday weekend!

FISH FROM GRIMSBY

Leading into the Low Level station from Station Street was an alley that was known as Chlppy Chase and this was where lorries backed onto to load the "PLA". Also off Station Street, a few steps further on, were two sizable wooden gates that gave access to the station, near a platform.

On the other side of the street was the "Fish Dock" - and every morning, Portsmouth's quota of fish arrived by rail direct from Grimsby. All local fish merchants would gather between 4.30am and 5am to pick up their required amount of fish.

"BLACK CAT" EXCURSION

One particular excursion that came into Portsmouth and Southsea Low Level on an annual basis, was the "Black Cat" cigarette factory train from the midlands. It was laid on for the benefit of its workers for their summer break.

When the excursion arrived, the workers stayed "under canvas" on the grass at Southsea Common, near a very popular walkway known as "Ladies Mile".

"OILER BOY" DUTIES

My work on the SR started in March 1943 as an "oiler boy" in the Carriage and Wagon Department at the Low Level station. Later, I was up-graded to an "adult oiler" and eventually as a "repairer" the latter entailed doing repair work on wagons at Fratton.

My duties then progressed to the title of "Carriage and Wagon Examiner" and this included examining and checking ALL parts of both steam and electric stock, and it included lighting, steam heating, brake adjusting, wheels and wheel flanges ... in fact it was a full full-time job. I got little leisure-time.

THE "MONKEY HOUSE"

Quite near the "Fish Dock" was sited a very large lock-up cage, and railway workers nick-named it "The Monkey House" directly opposite our mess and store room. This cage was used to store items of value, it was securely locked up.

CARRIAGE SIDINGS

Prior to the new power signal box being installed at the main station on the Canal Walk side, opposite its predecessor on the Greetham Street side there was a "third road" for berthing empty carriages, the other side of the main line were the DCS (Down Carriage Sidings). Later on these were changed to allow electric units to be kept there, when not in use.

COAL WAGONS "PUSHED"

The "Old Roads" sited between Fratton station and the tracks leading into the electric units shed, were mostly known for its coal delivery duties. The local coal merchants used to go there and they would hand shovel, bag and weigh their own coal requirements directly out of open-sided wooden railway wagons.

There was one particular duty that vividly stands out in my memory - this being when the loaded coal wagons were "pushed" by a Fratton allocated class "E4" 0-6-2 tank, from the "Old Roads" down to the DCS at Portsmouth and Southsea station (usually about 20 wagons) and the coal was destined for use at Portsmouth Electricity Power Station.

I recall that the shunter man used to sit up on top of the loaded coal wagon, leading with the waving of his red and green flags - he would then wave his green flag to the engine driver and away they would go! Health & Safety was virtually non-existent!

DOCKYARD TWICE A DAY

My railway duties took me into the Royal Naval Dockyard - two train loads of items were taken in, first was the 9.30 am train, second was the 2pm – both of these jobs had their return of wagons at about 11.30am and at 4.20pm. On these turns it was my responsibility to check the "in" and the "out" goods wagons, and making sure loads such as Gun Carriages which were used to carry 12" guns off berthed battleships in the Dockyard were secure.

The loaded wagons and its contents were then sent elsewhere for repairs.

A class "M7" 0-4-4 tank locomotive. This class was a Dugald Drummond design, and had a long life span. Fratton depot had a few in its allocation but they were withdrawn before Colin Robins was transferred from Yeovll depot (72C). Yeovil had Nos. 30129 and 30131, - primarily for the working of auto trains between Yeovil Town and Yeovil Junction.

COLIN ROBINS

An additional plus on my promotion to driver at Fratton locomotive depot was the shed staff, what a group of individual characters – trouble was, they would expect you to have a word even though it was obvious that duty called.

I was to spend many an hour in their company when spare, that is, not booked a running duty. There was one giant of a man that seemed to enjoy his adopted name of "Jumbo".

He had, we will say, "outside interests" – one was a bookies runner and another was anything second-hand. He obviously preferred night shifts.

I shall never forget the following gem, on a night shift involving "Jumbo" Collis: Fratton driver Fred Penfold and I was set in comfort with" Jumbo" in the signing-on office. The man in question was in charge as the shed foreman, as was the recognised habit, got his "head down" - (gone to kip).

There were at least four telephones on the desk, and Fred and I, both in our thirties, were out for a skylark. We decided to move the telephone hand-sets about so as their cradle's would not match. "Jumbo" did not suspect. Such was the anticipation of high jinks. Fred and I could not look each other in the face.

I remember, as if it was yesterday, "Jumbo" telling us to "bugger off" out of his office, to which we replied that we would keep quiet. "You'd better," was his threatening reply. This remark had me stuffing my handkerchief into my mouth. Fred was having silent convulsions. Christ! what's going to happen when the telephone goes off, keeps flashing across my eyes. It did! - we almost pressed the panic button and scarpered!

The hand-set on the correct phone was lifted, the voice uttered its usual "Wass up" which was appropriate - as at Fratton, especially at nights there was so many as we called them, "fiddles" taking place such as drivers with spare time doing the last part of fellow drivers duties so as they could, as we would say "Make yer way home mate, I'll do your last bit."

At times, even the best made plans would go wrong. Hence "Jumbo's" greeting of "Wass up". Now, back to the main gist – Fred and I are killing ourselves – the almighty lifts the other phone, still the wrong hand-set, Fred explodes, "Jumbo" scowls around, he's twigged us!

A full 18 stone, with fly weight steps wraps its hands either side of my shiny BR topped hat and pulls it down with such violence, that each side was lower than my ears! Meanwhile, Fred, crying with laughter, was lifted and slammed down on his feet and a size 12 boot helped his flying exit from the set stage – sorry, signing on office!

"Jumbo" Collis was well thought of by all grades ... What a character!

DAVE PALLETT

During my five years employed by SR which was first as a cleaner and then as a fireman at Fratton, then going out on loan to such sheds as Guildford and Nine Elms and even to Ryde (70H) on the Isle of Wight.

I became involved in many a prank, and one particular memory was the time that I had a shunters pole stuck through the arms of my overalls, and I was held up beneath a fully turned on water column - it was a very damp experience. Only consolation being, that it happened on a hot summers' day!

Talking about water, Fratton based men told me that the stories relating to the large water tower in the yard also had other uses, especially in the summer months was used as a swimming pool! It must have been quite refreshing after a hard day's stint on the footplate!

PLAY UP POMPEY

The most unusual events stemming from the water tower usually happened on a Saturday afternoon, why, you may ask on a Saturday? It would be quite common to see three or four men perched on the top edge of the watertank - they were getting a grandstand view of Portsmouth FC playing at the adjacent Fratton Park!

If the foreman was approaching, the code was three blasts on one of the steam engine's whistle in the yard, this told the football supporters to make a hasty retreat.

Obviously, there were also some sad memories, such as the day that I was fireman on the footplate of the last BR time-tabled passenger train to work between Hayling Island and Havant on the four-and-a-half popular branch line. The date was November 2 1963 and the leading steam locomotive was class "AIX" 0-6-0 "Terrier" tank No, 32662, and at the rear of the four carriage train was another class "AIX" No. 32650.

Being November, and the time was 10.35 pm - only the glow from the firebox and the lights on Havant station provided any chance for photographs, only a few were taken. A wreath to mark the sad occasion had been placed on the bunker of our engine, No. 32662. The train crew, which consisted of my driver George "Jock" MacAskill and the guard were met at Havant bay platform by porters Albert Grout and John Cherrison amongst many others, which consisted of railway enthusiasts.

Fratton based railwaymen had been very familiar with these diminutive tank engines as they, up until just before 1960 had been allocated to Fratton, then the depot was officially closed and they were re-shedded to Eastleigh. Both steam and diesels continued to use the Fratton facilities right up until July 1967.

GEORGE BLAKEY

My work on the railway started in July 1943 at Fratton locomotive depot. I recall that I went straight from school at the tender age of 14. This for me, was a bit of a culture shock, I had been thrown in at the deep end. At the end of the day there were about six locomotives in the shed building that were in for a boiler wash and other routine jobs, these had to be lit up for the early morning duties.

Now smoke from a fire in a cold boiler just rolls out the chimney until some heat is generated, thus giving a light draught on the fire - so the smoke then filled EVERY corner of the round house with fumes.

Prior to my starting work, the ravages of WW2 had left its mark on the shed roof, a class "T9" 4-4-0 No. 118 had a direct hit and was left in a sorry state with a large hole in the roof. Still on this theme, I believe it was a class "K" that had a bomb dropped on its tender, which not only left it flattened but it also seriously damaged the depots' coaling crane as well.

Luckily, there were no really serious injuries. My early days at the depot were virtually open to the elements following the visits of the Luftwaffe and I remember that one of the ways to keep warm was to saw and chop up some old sleepers that would be used for the engines firebox - another way to keep warm was to shovel sand into the drier, all these jobs especially in the winter months were welcomed.

Fratton had about 80 pairs of drivers and firemen plus support staff to maintain the 50 or so locomotives allocated. These were divided into links or gangs, the top gang consisting of 12 sets of men, these covered the majority of the passenger workings, Cardiff and Plymouth, these originated from Brighton, and Fratton men took over the controls at either Chichester or Barnham.

The much talked about "oil burners" came to light in 1946, this being in a bid to save coal after WW2, but it never really came to much, although numerous 4-4-0s, 2-6-0s and even some "King Arthur" and Bulleid "pacifics" were converted.

Many of the ancient classes were put on the "scrap line" but one Fratton class "U" 2-6-0 No. 31625 was converted back to coal – it is now in working preservation at the Mid Hants Railway - the "Watercress Line".

I was posted to the Middle East in 1947 and my National Service saw me at a Railway Operating Company, where LMS "8F" and "USA" 0-6-0 tanks were in use.

It was in 1951 that on the advice of my driver, Percy Osborne, that I should volunteer to transfer to Nine Elms in London, to give me some real experience, this coincided with the Festival of Britain season in 1951.

There were six Fratton railwaymen who took up this challenge, three going to Stewarts Lane (73A) with two others and myself going to Nine Elms (70A). We had accommodation provided for us in a railway hotel for the princely sum of one shilling per night. As the facility was right alongside of Charing Cross station, we had the enjoyment of the nightlife if we needed it. As it transpired us Fratton men spent ten months in London and it turned out to be one of the best times of my railway life.

I returned back to my local depot a much more knowledgeable railwayman.

OIL BURNERS FOR SCRAP

Before I conclude my Fratton "Memories" I have added the Fratton shedded class "T9" 4-4-0s that had been converted to oil burners, they being, in the early 1950s "stored" for scrap - they were as follows: Nos. 113, 114, 115, 118, 280, 303, 305, 314 and 731.

LEN WORBOYS

I had just turned 15 years old when I had an interview to become an engine cleaner at Fratton locomotive depot. The first thing manager Mr Smith asked me was "Do you support Pompey"? I instantly replied "Oh yes" to which he replied "Well, son, you can forget that as in this job you will be expected to work Saturdays as part of your shift"!

My wage was £2-10 shillings (£2.50) for a 48 hour week, and to work every other Sunday at overtime rate of time and three quarters. We had one rest day per fortnight - my hours were 6am-2pm, 8am-4pm and 2pm-10pm.

My mum was given £1-10 shillings (£1.50) per week for my keep, I had to clothe myself from the remainder. To get extra money, I virtually worked every Sunday!

My start of what was to be a 48 year job on the railway began on 28 December 1953, I joined ASLEF and I still remain so today.

My first impression of the engine shed was one of awe and some in trepidation, a place of oozing giant steam monsters, which was to become a part of my life. Going down the inspection pit below an "in steam" engine to clean the big end and webs etc. was scary and walls were painted red – a Mr Spencer, came to check our work, he had a spotless clean white cloth, he would rub the cloth over our work and if it showed any dirt, we had to repeat until he was satisfied.
The "fear" justification regarding close working with these monsters was brought to reality, when stores man Fred Somerset lost an arm when, as a fireman, he had been working in the inspection pit and the engine moved.

The depot manager a Mr. Smith, had just retired and was replaced by Mr Butler and I soon fell victim to his jobs he set me. One morning I was called into the office to be told that part of my duties would consist of polishing his office floor and to have a pot of tea ready for him on his arrival at exactly 9 am. Reluctantly, I took demand but it caused reaction from my mates which then set me on a course of action that almost cost me my job. To be called a "Creep"

was not too bad, but "Butler's Bum Boy" was over the top! My actions the next morning were to make his tea with cold tap water and to ensure that big splodges of red floor polish ended up on his black leaded fireplace! I then stood well clear at 9am and waited for the inevitable eruption – Butler went ballistic!

I told him that I was employed as an engine cleaner, and if he wanted an office cleaner he should employ one. This was witnessed by my fellow engine cleaners and I was under no illusion that I could well be sacked.

Mr. Butler said he would decide what action to take during the weekend. Monday morning came, and he said to me "So you think you're an engine cleaner Worboys - well, I'll show you what that job is really like." I was given an "A1X" 0-6-0 tank engine to clean - it was in a really terrible state and I was destined to spend 3 weeks of constant work to make it to perfection I escaped a sacking, but it was only through my fellow cleaners contacting the rule book that saved me.

I recall the shunting links, they were manned by the drivers that had failed their main-line driving medicals – this being mainly the eyesight test.

Firemen Ted Daish and Les Cooper took me under their wing, as they saw I was keen to progress - and I later became a passed fireman. One vivid memory that sticks in mind was the day Ted Daish got married to the depot canteen lady Joan Day. I was nearly 16 and I got very drunk – Ted had promised to keep an eye on me as he realised, over a period of time, that a degree of bullying had been applied. Joan had always treated me with respect, after finding me cowering outside of the canteen door with engine oil smothered over my nether regions - this being just one prank of bullying - this being my initiation! The wedding reception was held at the Wymening Arms, Cosham where I recognised driver Frank Lewington and Stan Webb, the others I did not know so I decided to make a swift exit.

The words "Come back you silly prat" rang out. Come and have a beer with us. Ted called me over and helped to make me most welcome. I will never forget that night for their kindness as did Stan Webb's wife Pat, although that was because I was sick all over her new dress!

My social life as a teenager during the mid and late 1950s was great fun to say the least. Back in those days, underage drinking of pints of Mild and Bitter was the norm, mainly because except for all lads over 18 were serving their National Service commitment.

We frequented the dance halls in Southsea, such as the Savoy, the Embassy and South Parade Pier - the latter being "RBN" - this was "Radio Band Night".

I worked with a bunch of dedicated railwaymen and was privileged to be part of the Fratton team in the depot team quiz nights. We were spurred on by Mr. Butler to win, and we became Southern Region Railway Quiz Champions in 1961. Then next year, our team broke up. At that date there were 19 firemen and I managed to become the youngest driver on BR at the age of 23.

After the 1955 strike an inquiry took place regarding pay and conditions and the outcome saw that electric trains were single manned and Motormen should receive more pay than a steam driver, who, of course double-manned. As time went by my job on the railway took me to London and then finally back to Portsmouth, to drive the electric unit trains.

SUNDAY WORK: time + three quarters.
REST DAY WORK: time + one half.
NIGHT WORK:
MILEAGE: extra pay for miles worked above 140, and escalating substantially for miles worked above 200.

In those days, train drivers basic pay was very poor, but it was supplemented by the above additional workings.

DOUG WILLIS

Although I lived only a short distance from Fratton engine shed, my duties as fireman emanated from Eastleigh (71A) - but that's not to say that some of my turns took me to Portsmouth.

I definitely recall a certain roster with my driver, when we had to run "light" engine from the depot into Southampton Docks, perform some shunting duties and then return "light" to Eastleigh shed.

We were given an Ivatt 2-6-2 tank to carry out the job, No. 41319. As the weather was cold we had the addition of a covered cab as we travelled bunker first via St. Denys to the docks.

Having negotiated our way in and had completed the shunting jobs we saw that we had time for a cup of tea and a sandwich before setting off home.

Our engine was next to a long line of vans and wagons, when a deep voice from down below in one of the wagons, bellowed "Do yah want any bananas mate"? The orange glow from our open firebox door revealed literally "hands" of bananas - "They're too over- ripe, and will have to be thrown away" came the message - "You can take what you want, and take some for the lads at Eastleigh" - we replied "Yes please". When we eventually got going, we had bananas all over the cab floor, in the coal bunker and put in every inch of space available.

After we had filled our lunch bags and stuffed the bananas into our overall pockets we handed out bunches for the depot staff - bicycle saddle-bags and scooter pannier bags were gratefully filled to bursting point. My driver and I had to get a "Hampshire" diesel to take us to Fratton, we were given some funny looks by passengers, as it was not easy to hide about 50 or so ripe bananas, it was obvious that our lunch boxes for the remainder of the week would consist of BANANA SANDWICHES!

This was just one of my many memories and antics that I and my fellow workers, encountered, but some others are best left un-printed!

COLIN CROMWELL

My association With Fratton Goods Depot took place between 1953 to 1964. The depot, off Goldsmith Avenue, came into being in 1936, originally sited just south of Portsmouth Town station, roughly where the Council offices are today. The official name, after its move to Fratton was Portsmouth Goods Depot.

The new location was a rather grand affair and was able to cope with all types of freight traffic, this being on a very large site on the eastern side of the engine shed. The administrative office block was in Goldsmith Avenue, and the Goods shed consisted of two enclosed tracks entering from the Fratton end, these tracks could cope with up to 24 standard open or van type wagons. The wagons opened onto a wide platform designed as a "U" shape with a roadway entering from the east - enough to allow trailer/vehicle loading bays adequate room to manoeuvre - the centre of this transfer platform was a single inset track, this ran the full length of the "U" as this was the pathway for an electric monorail crane.

Of note was that the Fratton end of the Goods shed had a higher roof area in order to provide a second floor which extended for nearly a quarter of its length - this was designated the warehouse section. It stored large amounts of products, that were subsequently delivered to local various outlets. The Kellogg Company were the largest users in the 1950s.

In the large yard were five sidings, all with adjacent road access, three of which ran the full length of the site, these used to load and off-load such items as ICI bagged fertiliser, frozen meat, bananas, machinery, crated sheet glass and beer in barrels that came from Burton-on-Trent!

I recall that the main freight services came from and to Eastleigh and Feltham, but there were individual wagons that came from all over the country - in fact, common carriers of ALL imaginable merchandise were handled and included personal effects, wines and spirits, non-perishable foodstuffs, china, and even bullion from the Royal Mint - you name it, the railway carried it!

Staff employed were roughly 200, including supervisors, working foremen, checkers, porters, drivers (road and crane), along with others such as clerical staff and engineers.

The Goods Depot ceased to exist as part of British Rail in the late 1960s, as did all others. On the 1 January 1969 the Transport Act (1968) was implemented, this created the National Freight Corporation and they absorbed many national road transport companies, it included freight handled by the railways, but with the exception of through bulk wagon trains, such as coal and oil.

GRAHAM BEECH

To conclude Chapter 9 a local railway enthusiast reveals the bonds that existed between railwaymen and train-spotters at Fratton depot - no such thing exists today, due to Health and Safety regulations.

Graham's story in his own words is brought to light: I resided less than a mile from the shed and I always considered Fratton as "my shed" having "bunked" it successfully so many times, but nevertheless being cautious both safety wise and being thrown out.

Two particular visits stand out in my memory, first was the night of Thursday 16 December 1965 when a friend and I entered the roundhouse about 6.30pm. On the turntable was Standard class "4" 4-6-0 No. 75077 - it was facing south, just then, the driver climbed down from the cab calling us over, and we both instantly thought we'd be ejected. But, to our amazement he said "When I shout, push on this lever – he shouted and we pushed but nothing happened for a few seconds, then the locomotive gathered speed until we had moved it through 180 degrees.

Finally the driver gave us a wave and the class "4" trundled out into the cold wintery night.

Secondly, 14 months later on Tuesday 7 February 1967, I entered the shed around 6.15pm where "West Country" class "pacific" No. 34006 *Bude*, minus its name-plates was simmering in the yard.   At this point I was chatting to another trainspotter (about my age, 17) - we were allowed to cab the engine, and after a brief chat, and to our sheer amazement, he opened up the regulator, we were in for a footplate ride to the top of the yard, or so we thought!

But no, the Bulleid "pacific" went out onto the mainline, it stopped short of Milton Lane footbridge for a points change. We then moved tender-first via the station avoiding line, a signal check was made.

Us two teenagers on the footplate staring at each other aghast, this indeed was an experience! We then had a three minute wait at Somers Road bridge. The glow from our engine's firebox fizzed around the crowded cab as we were given a "clear road" - and then, at my request, to the driver (his name was Les) - I was allowed to give a long blast on the whistle!

Finally, the engine backed onto the set of maroon parcel vans and other small vans at Portsmouth and Southsea (Low Level) station, the fireman coupled up to take the 7.06pm train to Eastleigh. We both thanked the driver profusely in allowing us a very memorable footplate ride.

The next night, once again it was the same locomotive and we had a repeat of the previous night, it was the same driver, but a different fireman. This time the fireman loaded his bicycle onto the footplate and gave me instructions to hold on to it. The usual signal checks were made prior to backing onto the parcel vans in the Low Level station. Looking back over the years, it seems impossible that two teenage spotters had an unforgettable experience, completely "out of the blue" that they would remember the rest of their lives. How times have changed!

Having seen this photograph of class "S15" 4-6-0 No. 30506 taken by Michael G. Harvey in 1958 in Fratton depot yard, it gave me the inspiration to reproduce it as an oil painting - it has been included on the front cover of this book. No. 30506 has been preserved on the "Watercress Line" in Hampshire.

CHAPTER 9

ERIC GRACE COLLECTION: PHOTOGRAPHIC GEMS!

The late Eric Grace was employed by British Railways from 1952 until 2002, he started off as a cleaner at Eastleigh depot, from where he moved to his local depot of Fratton, he then worked his way up the ladder to become a fireman and then a driver.

Between 1957 and 1967 Eric used his trusty Pentax camera to obtain photographs, not only at Fratton, but all over the country. The following photographs have been taken from his Portsmouth collection. I am most thankful to his widow, Ann Grace, for her permission to allow me to reproduce these marvellous collection of photographs. Some have been published in the "Railway Heritage - (Portsmouth)" book in 1997 co-authors Michael G. Harvey and Eddie Rooke.

ALL OF THE PHOTOGRAPHS COMPRISING OF CHAPTER 10 WERE TAKEN, DEVELOPED AND PRINTED BY ERIC GRACE.

One of Eric's favourite steam locomotive classes at Fratton depot was undoubtedly the "A1X" diminutive 0-6-0 tanks - known also as "Terriers" Fratton depot was their home depot until November 1960, when it was officially closed, but servicing of both steam and diesels continued up to July 1967 - when the final steam engine. departed from the depot yard.

Built in the 1870s, these sturdy engines had a very long life, ten out of the 50 built, still remain in preservation today.

These tank engines worked the nearby Havant to Hayling Island four-and-a-half miles branch line until November 1963, when a certain Dr. Beeching wielded his axe on this much loved line .. it is now just a memory.

To start Chapter 10 a selection of Eric's favourite steam locomotives at Fratton depot, the class "A1X" tanks, are shown.

ERIC GRACE

50
YEARS ON
THE RAILWAY
1952 - 2002

Having completed its daily duties on the Hayling Island branch, "Terrier" 0-6-0 tank No. 32636 has returned to Fratton depot, and is seen here inside the roundhouse. A July 1963 picture.

Two class "A1X" tanks pictured side by side in Fratton depot yard. Nos. 32650 and 32661. The building in the top background is the very large goods shed.   Demolished in 1995.

A work-stained "Terrier" tank engine. No. 32646 is quietly resting in the depot yard prior to its next duty on the Havant to Hayling Island branch.

Fratton depot yard in May 1963 with a brace of "Terriers" Nos. 32650 and 32678 being prepared for their duties on the Hayling Island branch. These tanks often travelled the six-and-a-quarter-miles to Havant in tandem, this being repeated on the return journey to Fratton, at the end of the day.

Class "A1X" 0-6-0 tank No. 32646 is photographed from an unusual angle, with a class "U" 2-6-0 in the foreground. The amount of goods vans (top) reflects how busy the goods traffic was at this date, 1962.

Front end view of "A1X tank No. 32661 in Fratton yard next to steam crane DS200. Note the spark arrestor fitted to the chimney, this being an essential addition, as the viaduct that crossed Langstone Harbour was constructed of wood.

Class "A1X" 0-6-0 "Terrier" tank No. 32670 was photographed in the sidings of the bay platform at Havant station - this is the arrival and departure platform when the "A1X" works the Hayling Island branch line. Note the footbridge (left) at the eastern end of the station, this station had TWO large footbridges, the other at the western end of the platforms, and they both survive today.

A wonderful picture of a "Terrier" 0-6-0 tank inside Fratton roundhouse in the early 1960s. No. 32650 is carrying a 71A shed-plate (Eastleigh Depot). A Standard class "4" is lurking in the background having just arrived and used the facilities in the yard.

FRATTON STATION SCENES IN THE MID 1950s

One of the elegantly designed class "D15" 4-4-0s No. 30468 awaits its departure from platform one at Fratton station with a passenger train for Southampton and Salisbury.

Class "N15" 4-6-0 No. 30745 *Tintagel* running "light" in reverse from Fratton depot. Note the "Southern" lettering on the tender.

This is a Marsh designed "Atlantic" 4-4-2 wheel arrangement locomotive No. 32425 *Trevose Head* departing from platform three at Fratton station, its next station will be Portsmouth and Southsea (Low Level) where it will terminate. Note the completely covered footbridge.

Just after passing under Milton Lane footbridge is a class "T9" No. 30313 of Salisbury depot (72B). It is slowing down as it approaches Fratton station. I think that this picture portrays the best views of the back yards of the terraced houses in Walmer Road. There are other pictures that include this background. Ironically, Eric Grace resided in one of these houses. Note the washing on the clothes lines.

FAREHAM

Class "D15" 4-4-0 No. 30471 at Fareham station with a train for Portsmouth.

COSHAM

Class "D15" 4-4-0 No 30472 approaches Northern Road bridge.

COSHAM

Western Region class "4900" (Hall) 4-6-0 No. 6927 *Lilford Hall* has just departed from Cosham. It is in a very smart condition. From information noted, this was the return passenger train from Portsmouth to Reading.

COSHAM

Fratton allocated class "K" 2-6-0 No. 32337 is running "light" westbound towards Fareham. WW2 prefabs form the background, this area today is know as the "Isle of Wight Estate" as streets are named after the IOW town names such as Freshwater and Sandown.

COSHAM

Eastbound freight train hauled by a class "S15" 4-6-0 No. 30510.

FARLINGTON

This is probably a Plymouth/ Exeter passenger train bound for Brighton – it is hauled by an unidentified class "U" 2-6-0. It is seen here passing the TWILFITS factory (right), note the factory name displayed on the grass area.

GOSPORT

Maunsell designed class "N" 2-6-0 No. 31411 is seen making its way down the Gosport branch line from the Fareham direction with a very long string of wagons.

"West Country" class 4-6-2 locomotive No. 34019 *Bideford*, takes a rest in Fratton depot yard. The unmistakable brick-built roundhouse forms the background. A 1961 photograph.

Standard class "3" 2-6-2 tanks were only occasional visitors to Portsmouth - here we see No. 82028 ambling past the former pump house building adjacent to the roundhouse in 1964. This class were comparatively new, as they were designed at Swindon in 1952.

Fratton steam driver L. Edwards finds time for a nice cup of tea in the cab of "West Country" class engine No. 34093 *Saunton* at Petersfield - this Eric Grace shot was taken on "Royal Duty" - it was awaiting to take the Queen Mother to London in May 1963. Eric would have been the fireman on this day.

Class "9F" 2-10-0 freight locomotive No. 92239 awaits its turn in Fratton depot yard to be coaled-up. This is a mid 1960s picture - No. 92239 would almost certainly be allocated to Eastleigh depot (71A).

This is an excellent Eric Grace shot of a Standard class "5" 4-6-0 in Fratton depot yard. Locomotive is No. 73110 named *The Red Knight*, - its home depot was Nine Elms (70A). A railwayman is placing an oil lamp (probably the fireman) whilst the driver, Brian Robey poses by the cab. A mid 1960s picture. This locomotive was given the above name-plates from class "King Arthur" 4-6-0 No. 30755 prior to it being sent to the scrap yard.

ERIC GRACE - AT THE SCENE OF MISHAP!

Above and below:
This Bulleid designed class "Q1" 0-6-0 freight locomotive has got itself into a spot of bother whilst working in Chichester sidings near the former Midhurst branch line. No. 33020 is an Eastleigh allocated engine. This particular locomotive was a very common sight at Fratton in the early 1960s. Railway workers from both Fratton and Brighton depots, were summoned to assist in getting the "Q1" back on the track. Note the Standard class "4" 2-6-0 (left).

Left: Shunted up against the buffer stop in the depot yard is Standard class "4" 2-6-0 No. 76063. Note the class "33" diesel (left) - this picture was taken on 3 July 1966.

Below: Close-up of the motion and cab of Standard class "4" No. 76061 - taken in 1962, both locomotives were allocated to Eastleigh.

Fratton depot yard in May 1963 was host to re-built "Battle of Britain" 4-6-2 locomotive No. 34088 213 Squadron, a Nine Elms allocation (70A). On this day, it was used on "Special Duty" from Portsmouth Harbour to London (Victoria). On the right are two Standard class engines, Nos. 73087 and 76016.

One of the Fratton allocated class "U" Maunsell designed 2-6-0s No. 31804, with a full tender of best Welsh coal, stands at the far end of Fratton yard ready for its next duty. A 1963 picture.

One of Eric's atmospheric photographs depicts some "Standards" lined up behind a "Terrier" 0-6-0 tank No. 32646 (right). Note the smoke-box door number plate of the "A1X' has had the black background painted over - a common alteration during the final years of steam operation.

Class "4" 4-6-0 Standard No. 75075 (carrying a 70D shed plate from Basingstoke depot) which was now to be Eastleigh's degraded code of 71A. This, and other degrading codes confused train spotters immensely! Note the line of coal wagons behind the tender; they were used to convey best Welsh coal from south Wales to Portsmouth at regular intervals, more are seen on the right with "16T" (tons) displayed. Fratton yard April 1964.

CLASS "C2X" 0-6-0 - WITH DOUBLE DOMES

Fratton depot had three of these quite unusual-looking class "C2X" 0-6-0 freight locomotives in its allocation. This picture shows No. 32549 (with double domes) quietly basking in the late 1959 sunshine on the siding next to the roundhouse. Also at Fratton were Nos. 32548 and 32550. This class was a Marsh rebuild of a Billinton design introduced in 1908. The Fratton "C2X" class could be seen employed on empty carriage duties between Portsmouth Harbour station and Fratton sidings. Other duties would be light pick up freight trains, taking wagons and vans at station sidings such as Havant, Chichester, Barnham, Bognor and Littlehampton.

A Bulleid designed class "West Country" 4-6-2 No. 34039 *Boscastle*, is taking a well earned rest in Fratton depot yard after hauling a Cardiff to Portsmouth train, which it took over at Salisbury. Picture taken, summer 1963.

This class "7" 4-6-2 main line steam locomotive was built to a Riddles design in the early 1950s, and, consequently, had engine, No. 70000 *Brittania* was saved for preservation, and it is used for enthusiasts specials up and down the country. London to Portsmouth Harbour station.

1 his axe. Luckily, this
ght a "Special" from

A typical Fratton engine shed yard picture, with a Standard class "4" 2-6-0 No. 76009 of Eastleigh depot, waiting to be coaled-up by steam crane number DS200, whose operator, "Jumbo" Collis, is seen here (right) having a sandwich prior to his next duty. The primitive iron containers were loaded with best quality coal taken from the row of wagons alongside of the crane. A mid 1960s picture.

A very smart-looking class "N" 2-6-0 locomotive No. 31831 probably ex-Works from Eastleigh has just taken on coal and water and awaits its next turn of duty. A mid 1960s picture.

Fratton yard is where this Standard class 2-6-0 No. 76011 is bound, after slowly making its way from the roundhouse building. Many engines in the early and mid 1960s, even though they had only a few more years life, were kept in a reasonably smart condition, as this picture shows. The evidence of a previous mishap is the new wall bricks at the entrance. April 1963.

Class "9F" 2-10-0s were a late addition to be seen in Portsmouth, they arrived on the scene in the early 1960s - being shedded at nearby Eastleigh, having been transferred from other depots. This Eric Grace picture of No. 92206, was snapped with his trusty Pentax camera in May 1963.

CLASS "K" - HIGHLY RESPECTED BY DRIVERS

One of the Billington designed class "K" 2-6-0s, No. 32349, a Fratton allocated engine, is in a very smart condition awaiting its next job. As can be seen, it is carrying a 71D shed-plate, this being the Fratton code prior to becoming 70F. Picture taken in 1957. There were three of this most delightful and elegant designed "K" class at Fratton, these being numbers 32337, 32347 and 32349. They were well respected by the Portsmouth drivers and firemen. Their duties included pick-up goods trains, empty carriage workings and the occasional local passenger train.

This is a 1962 photograph of class "West Country" 4-6-2 No. 34106 *Lydford* awaiting to use the facilities before its next turn of duty. The "West Country" and the "Battle Of Britain" class were most frequent visitors to Portsmouth, mainly having hauled passenger trains between Salisbury and Portsmouth, taken over from Western Region "Hall", "Grange", "Castle" or "County" classes, that had originated from Cardiff General and Bristol. They were also used on the "direct" line between London (Waterloo) and Portsmouth Harbour via Guildford and Petersfield.

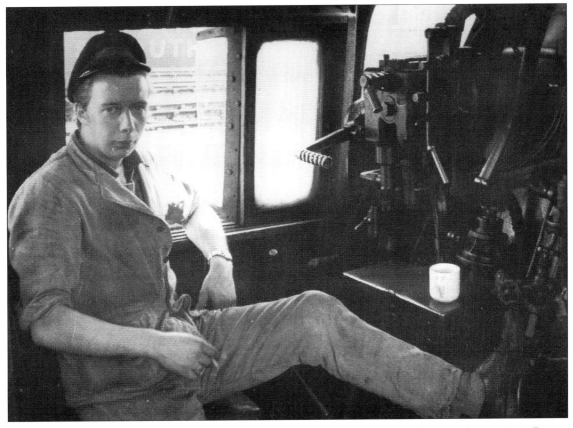

Fratton based fireman George Stevens rests with a cup of tea in the cab of an un-identified steam locomotive in Fratton yard, pictured in May 1965.

A 1961 photograph of Bulleid designed class "WC" (West Country) 4-6-2 No. 34027 *Taw Valley* in Fratton depot yard - its tender is waiting to be coaled by steam crane DS200. This locomotive had taken over a Cardiff General to Portsmouth Harbour passenger train at Salisbury. No. 34027 was one of the lucky locomotives to be saved for preservation, for future generations to savour.

Three "Terrier" 0-6-0 tanks Nos 32662, 32636 and one non-identified number. They are in the roundhouse on a late Sunday summer evening, having completed their stint on the Hayling Island branch. The "Terriers" returned to the depot in tandem via Bedhampton Halt and Hilsea Halt - this being the usual practice.

The date is 8 July 1965, and the weeds and vegetation have already started to take a hold in the depot yard - keeping company are two Standard class "4" 4-6-0s - Nos. 75069 and 75066. Note the double chimneys on both locomotives.

MINOR REPAIRS USING THE DEPOT HOIST

Class "A1X" 0-6-0 tank No. 32662 is undergoing some minor repairs. The brick built roundhouse forms the background. Any major repairs would have to be undertaken at Eastleigh Works.

Quietly tucked away on the station side of Fratton depot is Standard class "4" 4-6-0 No. 75066. This was a Basingstoke allocation. Its duties, along with other class "4" and class "5" 4-6-0s were quite regular on the Portsmouth to Reading passenger turns, via Botley and Eastleigh.

This class "4900" (Hall) 4-6-0 No. 4995 *Easton Hall,* was a most frequent visitor in Portsmouth, especially during the late 1950s and early 1960s. It would be noted hauling the weekdays passenger train from Reading General to Portsmouth & Southsea (Low Level) - its arrival time at Fratton (platform 2) was timed for 11.32, and it was very rarely late! It was a Reading a located locomotive (81D).

Fratton based railwayman John Tisdall is in the office of the depot foreman (Mr. Butler) and he is studying carefully his duties for the coming day.

Lawrence, J.	Mackay, C.
Simmons, K.	Bradbury, -
Terry, F.	Poat, T.
Bollents, T.	Rogers, A.
Carter, J.	Redman, R.
Penfold, F.	Lee, G.
Haywood, K.	Jones, P.
Tucker, G.	Covey, B.
Farmer, G.	Goodall, F.
Robins, C.	Moss, B.
Tisdall, J.	Chapman, W.

This list has been taken from Fratton depot roster board, near Mr. Butler's foreman's office. As can be seen, some familiar names appear in this mid 1960s list. Some names may be mis-spelt or initials wrong due to the much faded original copy.

These Bulleid designed class "Q1" 0-6-0s were quite common in Portsmouth. Most of them (40 in class) were allocated to Feltham, Guildford and Tonbridge. This is No. 33009 looking rather forlorn as it awaits its next duty. This 1963 photograph shows the depot roof caving in.

Ex-Works from Eastleigh: LMS class "4" 2-6-0 No. 43088. An Ivatt designed locomotive. This is a 1965 picture at Fratton depot.

On the 4 October 1964 Portsmouth railway enthusiasts saw No. 70000 *Britannia* at Fratton depot. It had been used on a LCGB "Vectis" rail tour emanating from London (Waterloo). On the right is Standard class "5" 4-6-0 No. 73022.

STEAM MEETS DIESEL AT FRATTON DEPOT - SUMMER 1963

"Steam meets diesel" at Fratton depot. On the left is Western Region class "Grange" No. 6812 *Chesford Grange*, and right, a class "33" diesel.

Diesel No. D5694 "on shed". It had just hauled an excursion from north London to Portsmouth Harbour. Steam crane DS200 is seen above the route indicator - didn't anyone inform "Jumbo" Collis that diesels do not require coal!

A Western Region diesel hydraulic locomotive meets up with a "Standard" class "4" 4-6-0 No. 75075.

Hey! . . . what have we got here? A group of Fratton loco men investigate some form of modern traction that had just arrived at the depot, after hauling an excursion from the west country to Portsmouth Harbour. In fact, it is a diesel hydraulic locomotive, and its creating some attention. Is that Eric Grace, with camera (right)? - probably, as he snapped up quite a few shots of this diesel. The caving in of the roundhouse roof tells you that the depot was near closing time in 1967.

In 1964 Fratton depot was host to a number of rarely seen classes - these locomotives would have been in ex-works condition, as they were used for "Running-In" turns following overhaul at nearby been Eastleigh Works. Here is one example, an LMS class "4" No. 43088. it was photographed near the north end of Fratton station. Its depot of allocation, at this date was Neasden (34E).

Class "WC" - Bulleid "pacific" No. 34104 *Bere Alston* is awaiting its turn to be coaled-up - it has very little coal in its tender. A summer 1963 picture.

A very smart looking class "9F" 2-10-0 freight locomotive No. 92239 has plenty of coal in its tender. It waits at the Goldsmith Avenue entrance of Fratton depot - note the familiar former pump house building forming the background. No. 92239 was at this date, summer 1963, allocated to Eastleigh depot (71A).

Here is one of Eric's photographs that he recorded the exact date taken. This being on the 5 September 1965. By this date, the majority of classes to be observed were of Standard designs, such as these, a class "4" 2-6-0 No. 76062 and class "4" 4-6-0 No. 75075. Note the zig zag roof of the large goods depot (left).

This is one of the Urie designed class "S15" 4-6-0s No. 30496 from Feltham depot (70B), no doubt awaiting to take on a northbound freight - as it's acquired a tender full of coal. These mixed traffic engines were introduced in 1920. This photograph taken in March 1962.

A summer 1963 busy scene depicting long-serving coaling-up crane operator "Jumbo' Collis he is seen depositing a container full of Welsh coal into the tender of an un-identified Bulleid "pacific".

Much interest was shown when a Western Region "Castle" class 4-6-0 locomotive No. 5050 *Earl of St. Germans* (82B) St. Philips Marsh allocation, found its way into Portsmouth with a school children's "Special" train from Bristol to Portsmouth Harbour in the summer of 1963. Eric Grace took numerous pictures, covering many different angles, some of his views are shown following this picture. As many railway enthusiasts already know, No. 5050 was immediately "Impounded" in Fratton yard for about three weeks, due to possible damaging of a platform at Fareham by this locomotive.

FOUR DIFFERENT CLASSES PHOTOGRAPHED AT THE DEPOT: EARLY 1960s.

Rebuilt class "West Country" 4-6-2 No. 34097 *Holsworthy* at the entrance to the roundhouse just prior to its taking on coal and water.

A Maunsell designed class "S15" 4-6-0 No. 30842 allocated to Feltham depot (70B) awaits its next duty.

This Bulleid designed class "Q1" 0-6-0 freight locomotive has only a coal wagon to keep it company. It is also a Feltham engine No. 33012.

One of the Fratton allocated class "U" 2-6-0s on the turntable - No. 31809.

Perfect picture from the Pentax camera of Eric Grace - Standard class "4" 2-6-0 No. 76010 awaiting its next job in the sidings at Fratton engine shed.   Photograph taken 8 August 1965.

Unusual angle of Fratton yard (looking towards the main lines. Picture taken from the top of the tender of a "Hall" class engine, a class "Q1" is directly above the chimney of the "Hall". Behind this is seen a class "4" Standard 2-6-0 that was working tender-first with a passenger train, heading out of Fratton. A late 1950s picture.

Right: Around this date (1957), the list of "on shed" locomotives were observed. As can be seen, quite an assortment of classes were present.

Jeff Wyncoll is snapped by Eric Grace at one of his favourite picture taking locations, just south of Basingstoke. Jeff was a very close friend of Eric Grace. He was a former steam driver from Fratton, and later a driver with South West Trains (on the Portsmouth to London (Waterloo) run via Havant, Petersfield and Guildford.

FRATTON SHED (7oF)
SUNDAY 21 JULY 1957

4912	BERRINGTON HALL	34005 BARNSTAPLE
4935	KETLEY HALL	34019 BIDEFORD
4987	BROCKLEY HALL	34051 WINSTON CHURCHILL
4994	DOWNTON HALL	34056 CROYDON
5933	KINGSWAY HALL	ALL WR LOCOS ON
6848	TODDINGTON GRANGE	EXCURSIONS
	30456 SIR GALAHAD	
30130	30787 SIR MENADEUKE	
30378	30788 SIR URRE OF THE MOUNT	
30300	31613	32650 (A1X)
30304	31629	32479
30707	31637	32509
30721	31638	32694 (E1)
30729	31801	73111/3/8
30730	31807	76005/8/9/12/14
30732	31809	76028/76063
75076	46 on shed	

WESTERN REGION "GRANGE" CLASS ON EXCURSION

No. 6812 *Chesford Grange* - former Pontypool Road allocation, but at this date (late 1950s) it was at Reading (81D).

Western Region "Hall" class 4-6-0s were more frequent visitors into Portsmouth, but the class "6800" (Grange) 4-6-0s (of a very similar design) could be seen occasionally, usually employed on Sunday excursion trains from the West Midlands, West London or South Wales areas. Local train-spotters could, from a distance, note the difference by virtue of the raised footplate above the cylinders.

This "Grange" brought in a Sunday excursion from the Reading area (late"1950s) Collett designed a class of 80 locomotives, basically for mixed traffic workings. Unfortunately, none were put aside for preservation - but in the early 1990s, railway enthusiasts deemed it possible to build a completely new class "6800".This work being undertaken at Llangollen in the late 1990s and later. The 80 locomotives that were introduced in 1936 were numbered 6800 to 6879.

The newly built example will carry the number 6880 and its nameplates will be *Betton Grange*.

The name-plate of the above locomotive is shown in close up. All Western Region named engines had their name-plates made of brass and to the same type face.

Class "7" (Brittania) 4-6-2 No. 70047 was the only one never given a name. It is seen here at Fratton depot in 1964 awaiting to take on water and coal, prior to working a return "Special" train.

Three steam locomotives of very different designs are captured in Fratton depot yard in this 1961 view. Left to right: class "A1X" 0-6-0 tank No. 32636, Standard class "4" 2-6-0 No. 76059 and "West Country" class 4-6-2 No. 34027 Taw Valley. No. 34027 has been preserved.

Class "4" Standard 4-6-0s were extremely common locomotives in Portsmouth during the period mid 1950s up to, and including July 1967. One of these is pictured in the yard at Fratton, No. 75070 on 3 July 1966. They were often observed hauling Portsmouth and Southsea (Low Level) passenger trains to Reading General via Eastleigh.

Pictured being coaled-up in the yard is a class "5" 4-6-0 Standard No. 73002 in the summer of 1962. It was not very often that locomotives from Weymouth depot were seen in Portsmouth.

Western Region class "4900" (Hall) 4-6-0 No. 6906 *Chicheley Hall* looking extremely smart, has been coaled up and watered ready before hauling a return Sunday excursion back to the West Midlands. This locomotive carries a 2D shed plate - home depot of Banbury. Note the reporting code 1X36 and the very clean white oil lamp fixed above the front buffer beam. An early 1960s photograph.

HAVANT AND HAYLING ISLAND STATIONS - MAY 1963

A double-header waits in the bay platform at Havant station, prior to hauling a three carriage train to Hayling Island station. "Terrier" tank No. 32646 leads an un-identified classmate. Note the luggage on the platform (right) and coal wagon (left).

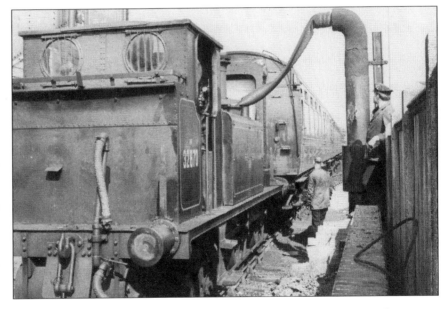

"AIX" 0-6-0 tank No. 32670 is taking on water at Havant station, this locomotive, unlike the one above, will work its train "bunker-first". The driver and fireman are making sure that the side tanks are filled up. The large fibre glass green livery carriages were higher than the steam engine, and when looking out of the window during the run, obliterated view of the engine. This was just one of the many features associated with this branch line.

Having arrived at Hayling Island station No. 32678 has been using the primitive method of talking on coal . . . by hand! It awaits departure from the station. The four-and-a half mile branch line had three stations, Langstone, North Hayling and Hayling Island. Journey time was just 13 minutes.

Hayling Island station view from the platform. The main building is on the right, whilst the goods shed is in the centre (with large roof). An "A1X" is next to the large deposit of coal which the fireman would have to refill the locomotive bunker by hand.

The branch line was closed in November 1963, one of the many Dr. Beeching "axe jobs".

VIEW FROM CAB OF AN "A1X" APPROACHING NORTH HAYLING

Marvellous portrait of class "BB" Battle of Britain "pacific" No. 34066 *Spitfire* resting in Fratton depot yard, awaiting its next turn of duty. This is a 1960 picture. No. 34066 was the locomotive involved in the Lewisham rail disaster on 4 January 1957. Although extensively damaged, it was repaired and was returned to working order for a few more years. Soon after the Lewisham disaster I, with a party of train-spotters from Portsmouth, visited Bricklayers Arms depot (73B) and saw No. 34066 - and by its condition, we were certain that it would be scrapped.

I think that the camera man must have been laying on the ground to produce this unusual angled picture of re-built "West Country" 4-6-2 No. 34009 *Lyme Regis!* Although not recognisable, this location is Fratton depot. Date May 1962.

An early 1960s shot of a local railwayman applying some minor repairs in Fratton depot yard on a "West Country" class 4-6-2 No. 34013 *Okehampton.*

Location of this picture is the Fratton depot foreman's office. The rather plump gentleman standing at the door is "Jumbo" Collis - the steam crane operator, amongst other miscellaneous odd jobs in the depot. "Jumbo" appears in quite a selection of Eric Grace's photographs, most of which are involved with DS200, the steam coaling-up crane. Mr. Butler was the foreman, and for us train-spotters trying to "bunk" the shed, he always seemed to catch us out! This is a mid 1960s photograph.

TWO LONG SERVING FRATTON RAILWAYMEN

This is Jack Neal, a Fratton driver and fireman complete with his grease top hat displaying the words "British Railways" on his badge. He seems to be a bit frightened by the camera. The locomotive is a Standard class "5" 4-6-0 named *Iseult*. (taken from withdrawn "King Arthur" class 4-6-0 No. 30749). A 1959 picture.

Stroudley LBSCR designed class "E1" 0-6-0 tank locomotive No. 32139 (note the 71D shed-plate), waits in the shed yard for its next duty. It was used on the Dockyard branch in the mid and late 1950s, along with class "O2" 0-4-4 tank No. 30207 and Fratton's other "E1" tank No. 32138. No. 32139 was sent to Eastleigh Works to be scrapped in the late 1950s. Date of picture is summer of 1957.

Depot yard tea break for the lads! Gathered round are three railwaymen in front of the concrete hut - far right is "Jumbo" Collis, whilst the others had such jobs as shunters or wheel-tappers in the adjacent "Field Sidings".

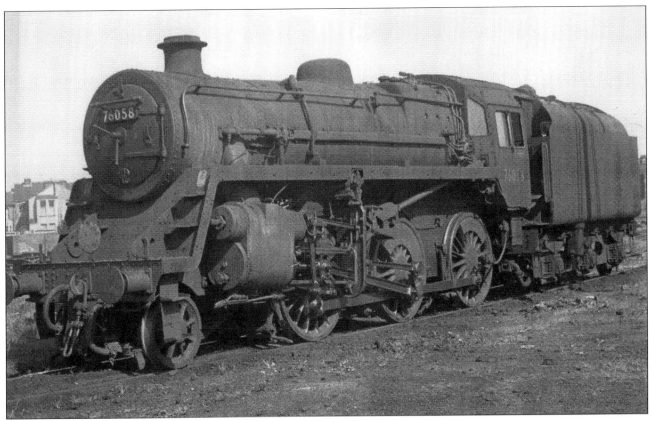

Note the high-sided tender fitted to Standard class "4" 2-6-0 No. 76058. Far left can be seen the backs of houses in Walmer Road, Fratton and ironically where Eric Grace lived for part of his 50 years employed on the railway. These houses form the background to numerous photographs that were taken in the depot yard.

No. 31853 is an "N" class "mogul" introduced in 1917, they were very similar to the "U" class "moguls" except that the "N" had 5 foot six driving wheels and the "U" were six inches larger. A "Q1" 0-6-0 is lurking behind No. 31853. Picture taken in early 1960s.

This is a "N" class "mogul" No. 31410 all alone on one of the Fratton depot sidings. Introduced 1928. Used on local passenger trains to Southampton, Salisbury, Eastleigh and Basingstoke, in later years they even worked the Portsmouth Dockyard turns. A 1962 picture.

Probably ex-Works from Eastleigh - this clean condition class "4" 4-6-0 No. 75016 is photographed in Fratton depot yard. It was former Nuneaton allocated, but sent to the SR following the phasing out of steam in the midlands. This is a 1962 picture.

A familiar sight in Fratton yard was these coal wagons. Although rather ancient-looking, the square iron containers that transferred the coal to the locomotives' tenders performed their job sufficiently. Note the assortment of goods vans in the background, and "Jumbo" is not very far away!

Quite a nice picture of a Standard class "5" 4-6-0 No. 73022 (a former midlands allocation) tucked away in a siding in front of Fratton depot roundhouse. The carriage, behind the tender, was the one kept at Fratton for emergencies such as derailments or collisions - it contained engineers tools and equipment relevant for these jobs. It was painted red, but by the end of steam in 1967, this colour had faded to a shade of pink! Also note, goods van behind the carriage, it also contained similar items. June 1963.

As mentioned in previous pages, the Western Region "Hall" and "Grange" mixed traffic locomotives could be seen in Portsmouth on a regular notings, especially during the summer months. This is a class "6800" (Grange) 4-6-0 No. 6857 *Tudor Grange*, seen on 25 August 1963 - it had hauled a ten carriage excursion from Wolverhampton to Portsmouth Harbour. On the left is a Standard class "4" 2-6-0 No. 76058, whilst behind the Grange is another Western Region 4-6-0.

A Drummond designed class "T9" 4-4-0 No. 30732 (of Fratton), is quietly resting by the roundhouse. They were a long lived class, this one was built in 1899 and scrapped in 1960. They could muster up quite considerable speeds. In earlier years they were used on Waterloo to Exeter passenger trains.

This is an Adams LSWR designed class "O2" 0-4-4 tank introduced in 1889. It was allocated to Fratton for many years, and found employment on station pilot duties at Portsmouth and Southsea station and often used to haul the twice daily goods vans and wagons to and from the Royal Naval Dockyard.

THREE MAUNSELL DESIGNED CLASS "Q" LOCOMOTIVES . . . FRATTON DEPOT AND CHICHESTER APRIL 1963

This "Q" class was allocated to Horsham depot (75D) - No. 30546 is awaiting its next duty at Fratton. Some of this class had acquired a wide diameter chimney, as this one.

The "Q" 0-6-0s were allocated to Eastleigh, Horsham, Three Bridges and Norwood Junction and others. Fratton workers shunted the sidings at Chichester, as did Brighton men. No. 30547 is seen at Chichester.

A total of just 20 class "Q" 0-6-0s were introduced in 1938 to a Maunsell LBSCR design. This is No. 30530 the first of the class. Noted in the depot yard.

Immaculate condition class "9F" 2-10-0 No. 92211 takes a rest in the depot yard, May 1963.

Side by side in Fratton depot yard - class "4" Standard 2-6-0 No. 76068 (71A) keeping it company is one of the 40 Bullied designed class "Q1" 0-6-0s No. 33004 of Guildford depot (70C).   Mid 1960s.

Fratton allocated class "E4" 0-6-2 tank No. 32505 - with a 71D shed-plate. This mid 1958 picture finds it in spotless condition. Their duties at Fratton included shunting the Field Sidings and empty carriage workings, taking carriages to and from Portsmouth Harbour station. This class introduced in 1921.

During the summer timetable, Monday to Saturday, a steam-hauled passenger train ran from Reading General to Portsmouth and return usually hauled by a Western Region "Hall" class 4-6-0. Here is No. 5983 *Henley Hall* on this duty - which always arrived at Fratton station platform 2 at 11.32am. The return journey departed from Portsmouth in mid afternoon."Hall" No. 4995 *Easton Hall*, was a Reading (81D) allocation, and it also made countless appearances on this particular train.

A mixed freight train is seen about to pass under Milton Lane footbridge and into Fratton sidings. The locomotive is a class "N" 2-6-0 No. 31410. St. Marys Road bridge is in the background. May 1962.

Date is 18 October 1960 and the steam locomotive is a Standard class 2-6-4 tank No. 80082 quietly simmering away - it is in the siding where the red breakdown carriage (DS 232) is kept.

This appears to be a minor derailment involving a Standard class "4" 2-6-4 tank locomotive whilst shunting wagons in Chichester sidings. Rail workers would have been summoned from Fratton to assist those from Brighton with a lifting crane. A mid 1960s photograph.

Another angle of the derailed wagons in Chichester sidings. The rough location of this incident was west of the station, where today diesels are employed hauling wagons of stone from the west country.

No. 73014 a Standard class "5" 4-6-0 in Fratton yard awaiting its next job. This particular locomotive was allocated to Shrewsbury (84G), when Eric Grace took this picture in April 1962. This class were designed at Doncaster Works and Introduced in 1951.

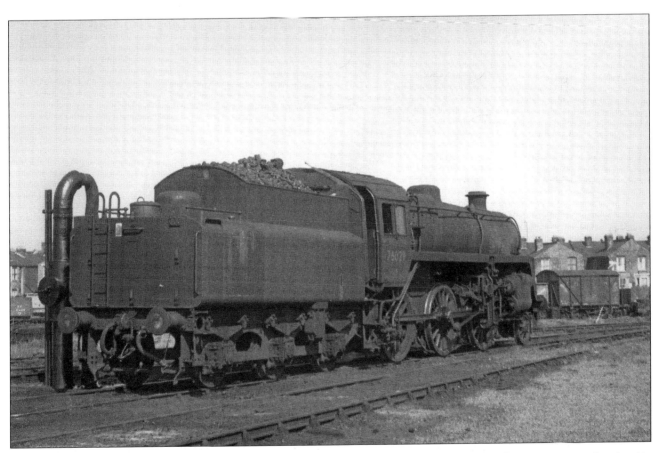

A tender-first photograph of Standard class "4" 2-6-0 No. 76029 (of Eastleigh). As can be seen, it has taken on its quota of coal and is ready to depart from the depot yard. There were always many vans and wagons in the vicinity of the yard, some are seen in this view, with Walmer Road in background.

Ex-works from Eastleigh, rebuilt class "MN" 4-6-2 No. 35007 *Aberdeen Commonwealth* is next to be coaled-up by steam crane DS200. Locomotives often made "running-in" turns, such as this one, prior to being returned to their home depot. Summer 1964.

Bulleid designed class "Q1 " 0-6-0 No. 33039 of Feltham depot - takes a rest In Fratton yard. There were 40 of these most unusual designed locomotives introduced at the outbreak of WW2. Nick-named "Charlies". Their aim was to provide a basic steam engine to haul war time freight trains. Note the lack of running plate, and the easy access to motion intended for freight work only, they were, in later years, sometimes found hauling local passenger trains. No. 33001 has been preserved. Mid 1960s picture.

Portsmouth railwaymen never did get to see this, famous steam engine No. 4472 *Flying Scotsman*. The nearest that it came was Bedhampton Halt and Cosham, the former being the location of this picture. The date is September 1966. It was hauling a "Special" eight carriage train departing from London (Victoria) to Eastleigh via Chichester, Havant and Fareham.

TWO "U" CLASS 2-6-0s IN FRATTON YARD: 1960

Fratton allocated "U" Class No. 31637. The engine was scrapped but several of its sisters survived courtesy of the scrapyard at Barry and No. 31638 is preserved at the Bluebell Railway in Sussex.

Another Fratton allocated class "U" No. 31805. This one was not so lucky, it was sent to the scrap yard.

A "backside" view of the fireman performing one of his dusty duties, cleaning out the ash from this class "Q" smoke box. June 1963.

Having brought in a passenger train from Salisbury, class "BB" (Battle of Britain) 4-6-2 No. 34054 *Lord Beaverbrook* awaits its next duty in Fratton yard. It had taken over from a "Hall" class 4-6-0 which had hauled a passenger train from Cardiff General. A September 1961 picture.

ENGINE DRIVER'S VIEW FROM CAB

This is the view that Eric Grace sees from the cab of the class "A1X" 0-6-0 tank as it approaches Havant station. May 1963.

This unusual picture was obtained by climbing onto the footplate of Britannia class 4-6-2 No. 70047. Intention was to photograph its chime whistle. No. 70047 was the only one of its class not to carry nameplates. It brought an excursion into Portsmouth Harbour station in the mid 1960s. Hidden in the shadows (right) is a Standard class "5" 4-6-0.

Class "A1X" - "Terrier" tank 0-6-0 No. 32670 has just had its coal bunker filled - together with a sprinkling of coal on the cab roof! This was an early morning picture, as it waits in Fratton yard for a second "A1X" to join it and then make their way in tandem to Havant to work the Hayling Island branch.

SOME WESTERN REGION STEAM LOCOMOTIVES AT FRATTON DEPOT: SUMMER 1962 & 1963

Eric Grace took numerous pictures of "Castle" class 4-6-0 No. 5050 *Earl of St Germans* during its visit to Fratton in the Summer of 1963 - this is a close-up of a cylinder and the leading bogies.

"Grange" class 4-6-0s were occasional visitors to Fratton, but to capture TWO of this class together in Fratton yard was a complete rarity! Both had brought in separate Sunday excursions during the summer of 1963. The locomotives were Nos. 6842 *Nunhold Grange* and 6846 *Ruckley Grange*.

Front end view of class "6959" (Modified Hall) 4-6-0 No. 6996 *Blackwell Hall*. This is a summer 1962 picture. Note: the yard was probably full of engines, as this one had been placed between two lines of wagons. It carried a reporting code above its front number plate "1X 06".

No. 5050 AT FRATTON 1963:

Another one of that "impounded" "Castle" class 4-6-0 No. 50S0 *Earl of St. Germans*.

This was the most photographed steam not only by Eric Grace, but also by the local train-spotters during the summer of 1963.

The railwayman in the centre foreground of this picture is Fratton based fireman R. Horman. He is checking the wagons at Eastleigh prior to working forward to Basingstoke with the 4.15pm ex-Fratton. The time is 5pm on 3 September 1965. This view was taken from the cab of a re-built "West Country" class 4-6-2 No. 34108 *Wincanton*. The station is in the distance looking north, but is partially hidden by one of the oil wagons.

PART OF MOTION OF STANDARD CLASS "4" 4-6-0

This close-up section of a steam locomotive belongs to Standard class "5" 4-6-0 No. 75079 It is awaiting restoration today at the Mid Hants Railway "Watercress Line" in Hampshire.

ROUNDHOUSE IS IDEAL HAVEN FOR STORED STEAM LOCOMOTIVES PENDING PRESERVATION

MID 1960s: We saw numerous "Special" steam-hauled rail tours, not only in the Portsmouth area, but also all over the country. The examples below show just a few "foreign" types that appeared with enthusiasts' tours, in the Portsmouth area during these years.

Two complete strangers to the south coast, seen on the Coastway West route were former LNER (London and North Eastern Region) locomotives lovingly restored for private preservation following their withdrawal by BR - these sporting an apple green livery of their original owner. The first of the two locomotives in question ran on Sunday 17 September 1966 and was hauled by the World famous "pacific" No. 4472 *Flying Scotsman* employed on a London (Victoria) to Eastleigh tour via Hove, Chichester, Havant, Cosham and Fareham.

Six months later, on Sunday 12 March 1967, we had the pleasure of seeing class "K4" 2-6-0 No. 3442 *The Great Marquess* - it took a similar path to reach Southampton and then returning from Eastleigh via Cosham, and along the Coastway West route.

No. 3442 appeared to be the very LAST BR steam locomotive to work westwards between Brighton and Portsmouth under its own steam and then the LAST to run eastwards along this coastal route.

To end Eric Grace's Chapter 10 - now follows a selection of his photographs (still with his trusty "Pentax" camera) of some of the ex-British Railways steam locomotives that were lucky enough to be stored at Fratton depot, pending possible preservation. The mid 1960s saw many more ex-BR steam put aside for preservation.

It proved to be a safe haven, with the added security of a roof, although by 1967 even that had succumbed to the ravages of time! The majority of those locomotives that were present were towed away by class "33" diesels. The bulk were towed first to Stratford Works and then later moved on to Brighton (Preston Park) in the early 1970s.

Other redundant steam were towed away from their depots to the scrap yards of South Wales, stopping off at Salisbury depot yard en route. Class "33" diesels were used for this duty.

STEAM LOCOMOTIVES "IN STORE" AT FRATTON

Drummond designed class "T9" 4-4-0 No. 120 inside Fratton roundhouse, already preserved, but waiting a location for its safe keeping. 1963.

ALL LINED UP FOR A PHOTOGRAPH (from left to right)

Classes "0298" 2-4-0 No. 30587, "Schools" 4-4-0 No. 30926 *Repton*, "LN" 4-6-0 No. 30850 *Lord Nelson*, "Schools" 4-4-0 No. 30925 *Cheltenham*, "N15" 4-6-0 No. 30777 *Sir Lamiel* and "M7" 0-4-4 tank No. 30245

STEAM LOCOMOTIVES "IN STORE" AT FRATTON

"NIS" (King Arthur) class 4-6-0 main-line locomotive No. 30777 *Sir Lamiel*, with its nameplates removed together with many other parts. It had a happy ending, it was towed away to be put aside for preservation. It is now in working order. No. 30777 was built by the North British Locomotive Company in 1925.

STEAM LOCOMOTIVES "IN STORE" AT FRATTON

The "Schools" class, comprising of 40 locomotives, numbered 30900 to 30939. were the most powerful 4-4-0 wheel arrangement types in Europe. No. 30926 *Repton* bides its time in Fratton roundhouse in 1963. It was saved for preservation. Left: visible. is class "0298" 2-4-0 Beattie well tank No. 30587.

Shafts of sunlight filtering through the remains of the shed roof reflects on the line up of steam pending preservation. The locomotive, third from left, was a class "Q" 0-6-0 No. 30538, it was not so lucky, and was cut up for scrap in the mid 1960s.

STEAM LOCOMOTIVES "IN STORE" AT FRATTON

One of the rarest Southern Region steam engines ever to visit Fratton depot was this class "Z" 0-8-0 heavy tank No. 30952. It was designed by Maunsell and introduced in 1929. Here we see it resting in the roundhouse awaiting to be towed away for scrap. It was thought that the Bluebell Steam Railway were keen to purchase it for preservation, but this did not materialise, due to lack of funds at that date. This picture was taken in 1963 and it lingered on for a short time and then eventually it was towed to Cashmore's scrap yard at Newport, south Wales in January 1965 and cut up. It would have been an interesting addition at one of today's preserved steam railway centres.

Drummond designed class "M7" 0-4-4 tanks were an everyday sight on the Southern Region including Fratton. Their duties included light passenger workings, station pilots and empty carriage duties. In this Eric Grace picture we have No. 30245 and it was luckily put aside for preservation for future generations to savour. No. 30245 spent most of its long life allocated to Barnstaple Junction depot in north Devon from where it worked the local branch lines.

Beattie well tank 2-4-0 No. 30587 is safely tucked away from the elements in Fratton roundhouse pending its preservation.

STEAM LOCOMOTIVES "IN STORE" AT FRATTON

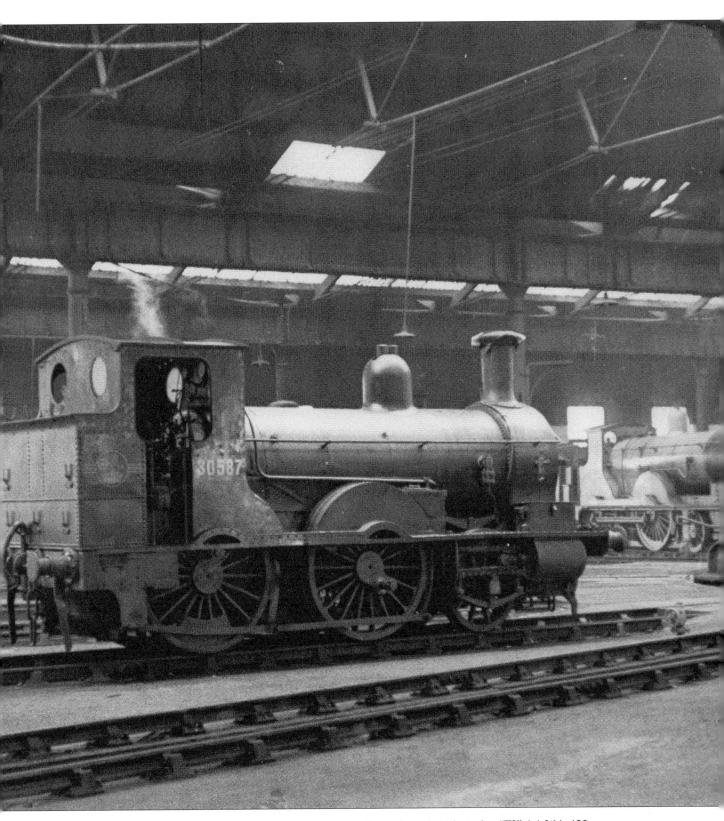

Another angle of Beattie well tank No. 30587 (with tarpaulin over its chimney) on the right is class "T9" 4-4-0 No.120.

STEAM LOCOMOTIVES "IN STORE" AT FRATTON

Fratton proved to be a safe haven for storage of ex-BR steam - on the left is a class "Q" No. 30538 unfortunately, this Maunsell designed locomotive was not preserved - but class "V" (Schools) 4-4-0 No. 30925 *Cheltenham*, awaits to be towed away for restoration for future generations to savour.

STEAM LOCOMOTIVES "IN STORE" AT FRATTON

Class "LN" 4-6-0 No. 30850 *Lord Nelson* is coupled to class "N15" 4-6-0 No. 30777 *Sir Lamiel*, note both have tarpaulins over their chimneys. Their nameplates, connecting rods and shed plates have all been removed for safe keeping. It is now mid 1960s as the pair await to be towed away from Fratton to Stratford Works, and later Preston Park (Brighton).

STEAM LOCOMOTIVES "IN STORE" AT FRATTON

This is the only class "T9" 4-4-0 out of a class of 50 that has been restored to preservation standard. It was introduced in 1900 to a Drummond design. Stored at Fratton prior to it being transferred to one of Britain's Railway Heritage locations and return to working order.

NOTE: PAGES 111 to 118 DISPLAY FURTHER STEAM PHOTOGRAPHS TAKEN AT FRATTON. THESE DO NOT INCLUDE "IN STORE" LOCOMOTIVES.

Fratton shed had the distinction of a visit by the sole un-named "Britannia" class locomotive No. 70047. The date being 1963 - it had hauled a "Special" excursion train, terminating at Portsmouth Harbour station. Built at Crewe Works in 1951.

A close up picture of Merchant Navy "pacific's" nameplate and flag belonging to No. 35007

No. 35007 *Aberdeen Commonwealth* in Fratton yard - it was on a "running-in" turn, following overhaul at Eastleigh Works in 1964. The running-in turn from Eastleigh to Fratton was an ideal distance (about 50 miles return) to locate any additional work that might be needed before the overhauled locomotive was returned to its depot of allocation. The engine is a re-built class "MN" (Merchant Navy) pacific.

Maunsell designed class "N" 2-6-0 locomotive No. 31411 was a "mogul" that Eric Grace often fired and drove - it is seen here awaiting its new duty. An April 1960 picture.

HIGHLIGHTING THE CHIME WHISTLE ON No. 70047

Eric certainly found those unusual angles to add to his collection, this being a prime example, the chime whistle of "Britannia" class 4-6-0 No. 70047, or was he highlighting the object appearing from the locomotives' chimney? Note the familiar background once again of the houses in Walmer Road - these being included in numerous pictures when looking towards Fratton East signal box.

Class "A1X" 0-6-0 tank No. 32650 is being hand coaled in the sidings at Hayling Island station. The fireman is standing just to the left of the coal bunker. The four-and-a-half mile branch line was closed by Dr. Beeching in November 1963.

Re-built class "WC" (West Country) "pacific" No. 34009 *Lyme Regis* in Fratton yard. It is waiting to use the facilities. From the roofless roundhouse, it tells you that this was a mid 1960s picture.

ONE LARGE AND ONE SMALL
Here is the marvellous view that Eric had, photographed from the cab of a class "A1X" as it slowly crosses Langstone viaduct. 1963.

This is the nameplate and badge of West Country" class "pacific" No. 34004 *Yeovil*.

ONE LARGE AND ONE SMALL
Cab view from "A1X" as it nears the A27 road bridge at Havant. The track is today a part of the
Hayling Billy walkway and cycleway.

Standard class "4" 4-6-0 No, 75066 keeps company with a class "4" 2-6-0 No. 76010.   Date of this picture was April 1965.

ONE LARGE AND ONE SMALL
This is the final view from the cab window of a class "A1X" as it enters the bay
platform at Havant station having completed its four-and-half miles branch line run
from Hayling Island station. 1963.

CHAPTER 10

DRIVERS AND FIREMEN AT FRATTON

THIS LIST CONTAINS THE NAMES OF DRIVERS AND FIREMEN THAT STAN WEBB CAN RECALL FROM THE YEAR 1942.

STAN WEBB JOINED THE SOUTHERN RAILWAY ON 31 MAY 1942, AND WAS BASED AT FRATTON LOCOMOTIVE DEPOT. IT WAS AN IMMENSE TASK COMPILING THIS LIST AND, NATURALLY SOME NAMES MAY BE MISSING.

Thanks to Fred Somerset and Sandy Hayward for their help, I hope the above brings back happy memories of years long ago on the footplate.

I ABRAHAMS J	32 BOOTH JOHN	63 COLE T	94 EDWARDS TAFFY (SOT)
2 ALLEN FRED	33 BOSWELL JACK	64 COLLINS DES	95 ELLIOTT ALBERT
3 ANDERSON W	34 BOYCE LES	65 COLLINS GEORGE(SNR)	96 ELLIOTT GEORGE
4 ANSTEY JACK	35 BOYLAND(JINGLE)	66 COLLINS GEORGE(JNR)	97 ELLIOTT JIM(G-POR
5 ARMSTRONG ROY	36 BOYS TOM	67 COLMER BILL	98 ELSTON JACK
6 ATKINS ALAN	37 BRADBURY HARRY	68 COLLIS GEORGE	99 EVANS HARRY
7 ATKINS JOHN	38 BRADBURY PETE	69 COMBEN FRED	100 FARLEY RON
8 ATTRAY RALPH	39 BRADBURY VIC	70 COOKE ALBERT	101 FARMER CYRIL
9 AULT (GINGER)	40 BRAKE ALF	71 COOPER HARRY	102 FELLOWS PAUL
10 AVIS RAY	41 BRAME JOHN	72 COVEY NIGEL	103 FELLOWS SID
11 AYLING ALF (Snr)	42 BREWER JACK	73 COX BRIAN	104 FERRIS RON
12 AYLING ALF	43 BREWER ROY	74 CRAWFORD BILL	105 FENTON FRED
13 BAILEY BERT	44 BROWN ALF	75 CREASEY JIM	106 FEW SID
14 BAILEY GORDON	45 BROWN PETE	76 CRISELL ALF	107 FINCH KEN
15 BARBER BILL	46 BUNN GEORGE	77 CUMMINGS LES	108 FOOT ALBERT
16 BAKER BILL	47 BURTON HARRY	78 DAISH TED	109 FORD JIM
17 BAKER LOU	48 BURTON LEN	79 DAIVE DICK	110 FORDER RAY
18 BARNETT JACK	49 BUCKWELL TERRY	80 DAVEY CECIL	111 FRENCH D
19 BARRIBALL JIM	50 BURGHARD JACK	81 DAVEY STAN	112 GARNETT FRED
20 BATH GEORGE	51 CALDWELL JOE	82 DAVIES GARY	113 GARRARD JIM
21 BEARD DENNIS	52 CAREY JOHN	83 DAWSON ALF	114 GIBBS JOHN
22 BEDFORD HARRY	53 CAREY PHIL	84 DAWSON JACK	115 GODDARD GEORGE
23 BILES BERT	54 CARPENTER STEVE	85 DOLLERY ERN	116 GODDING ERN
24 BIRCH DAVE	55 CARTER JIM	86 DOUGHTY CLAUDE	117 GOLDSWORTHY BERT
25 BLACKLER LES	56 CHANDLER LEN	87 DOWNES STAN(MPO)	118 GOSNEY SID
26 BLACKLER WALLY	57 CHAPMAN CHARLIE	88 DREW-READING LEN	119 GRACE ERIC
27 BLAKEY GEORGE	58 CHAPMAN ROY	89 DUBB GRAHAM	120 GRAINGER BILL
28 BLENCOE FRED	59 CHARLTON BOB	90 DUBB LEN	121 GREANY TERRY
29 BOLGER TOM	60 CHICK RON	91 DURANT BILL	122 GREEN JIMMY
30 BOND TED	61 CLEAL ERN	92 EAYRS MICK	123 GREEN STAN
31 BOOKER GEORGE	62 CLEAL FRED	93 EDWARDS LEN	124 GREENFIELD WALTER

125 GRIFFIN HARRY	165 JONES KEN	205 MIDDLETON G	245 PENFOLD FRED
126 GRIFFIN TONY	166 JOSHUA ERIC	206 MILES LES	246 PERCY (M-HURST)
127 GROIZARD BOB	167 KEELING PETE	207 MILLER COLIN	247 PERKIS JOHN
128 GULLIVER FRED	168 KIMBER BILL	208 MILLS GEORGE	248 PETERS GEORGE
129 HABERSHON RON	169 KNAPP RAY	209 MINTRAM HARRY	249 PHILLIPS BARRY
130 HALL HARRY	170 LADD WALLY	210 MITCHELL BILL	250 PICKETT ERN
131 HALL MICK	171 LAISHLEY KEN	211 MOREY TED	251 PINNOCK GEORGE (SNR)
132 HALL WALLY	172 LANGRIDGE TOM	212 MORRISON LES	252 PINNOCK (JNR)
133 HALLAM RON	173 LAWRENCE JACK	213 MOSS BRIAN	253 PITCHER JACK
134 HARTFREE JOHN	174 LAWS HARRY	214 MOWATT BOB	254 PITMAN GEORGE
135 HARTLEY CHARLIE	175 LAYTON ALAN	215 MUNN JACK	255 PITMAN RON
136 HASTINGS (JOCK)	176 LEATHLEY JACK	216 NEAL CHARLIE	256 PLANT DAVE
137 HAWKINS FRED	177 LEE MICHAEL	217 NEAL JACK	257 POAR TERRY
138 HAYES TED	178 LEESON JOE	218 NEW TED	258 PORTER BERT
139 HAYLES BILL	179 LEWINGTON FRANK	219 NEWELL GEORGE	259 POWER DAN
140 HAYWARD SANDY	180 LEWIS DES	220 NEWMAN FRED	260 POWER KEN
141 HAYWOOD KEN	181 LILLYWHITE JOHN	221 NEWPORT TOM	261 PRAGNELL REG
142 HEARD T	182 LINSDELL CHARLIE	222 NEWTON BERT	262 PRICE GEORGE
143 HEASMAN CHARLIE	183 LITTLEFIELD SID	223 NOKES TED	263 PRIVETT J
144 HEATH HAROLD	184 LLOYD JACK	224 NOLAN JOE	264 PUDDICK CHARLIE
145 HENDERSON DON	185 LLOYD JOHN	225 NOLAN FRANK	265 RANCE TOBY
146 HESLOP FRED	186 LLOYD REG	226 NORRIS A	266 RAND(KILLED AT CHI)
147 HICKMOTT TED	187 LOBB ALF	227 OLIVER FRED	267 RAPSON NORMAN
148 HILL CHARLIE	188 LOCKE CHARLIE	228 ORCHARD JACK	268 REDDIND JOHN
149 HOLCOMBE FRED	189 LOFTING ALF	229 OSBORNE ARTHUR	269 REDMAN BOB
150 HOLLANDS TOM	190 LUTER KEN	230 OSBORNE FRED	270 REDMAN GEORGE
151 HOLYOAK BILL	191 LYDE BOB	231 OSBORNE PERCY	271 RIGLER BOB
152 HOLYOAK CYRIL	192 MABEY GERALD	232 OUTEN HARRY	272 ROBINS COLIN
153 HOOPER RON	193 MACKLEY DAVE	233 OXFORD LEN	273 ROBINSON JOE
154 HOPGOOD HARRY	194 MANSELL HARRY	234 OXFORD LOU	274 ROBY BRIAN
155 HULLAND RON	195 MARLEY JIM	235 PACK BOB	275 ROBY COLIN
156 HUNT FRANK	196 MARSHALL ALF	236 PALMER HARRY	276 ROGERS CLIFF
157 HUXTABLE JOHN	197 MARSHFIELD JOHN	237 PARKER REG(SNR)	277 ROGERS GEORGE
158 HYSON BERT	198 MATTHEWS DAN	238 PARKER REG(JNR)	278 ROGERS NORMAN
159 JAMES R	199 MAY IVAN	239 PARKIN SAM	279 RUSSELL ALAN
160 JEFFREY DON	200 MERIDITH HARRY	240 PAVEY JOE	280 RUSSELL CHARLIE
161 JEFFRIES (SNOWY)	201 MERRITT BILL	241 PAYNE GEORGE	281 RUSSELL C.P.
162 JENNINGS JACK	202 MCASKILLE (JOCK)	242 PEACOCK ALF	282 SALTER FRED
163 JONES ALF	203 MCKENZIE DON	243 PALLETT RICKY	283 SAMPSON PETE
164 JONES BRIAN	204 MCNAMARA DON	244 PALLETT DAVE	284 SANDELL BILL

285 SEARLE JOCK	325 TUCKER FRED	365 WILLIAMS CHARLIE
286 SESSIONS BRIAN	326 TUCKER GEORGE	366 WILLIS C
287 SHEPPARD DEN	327 TURNER BILL	367 WITHERS JOHN
288 SHERWOOD HARRY	328 TURNER RON	368 WITT GEORGE
289 SIMMONDS KEN	329 TURTLE RON	369 WITTCOMBE GEORGE
290 SKINNER FRANK	330 VALLANCE RON	370 WOODS WILLIE
291 SLOAN FRED	331 VICKERY GEORGE	371 WOOLMINGTON REG
292 SOFTLEY LEN	332 VINEY JACK	372 WORBOYS LEN
293 SOMERSET FRED	333 VINEY MALCOLM	373 WRIGHT BERT
294 SOMERSET WALLY	334 WAKEFORD LEN	374 WYNCOLL JEFF
295 SOPER CLAUDE	335 WALDRON JIM	375 YALDEN BILL
296 SPRAKE JOHNNY	336 WALLACE JIM	376 YOUNG HAROLD
297 STAPLETON DOUG	337 WALLACE VIC(SNR)	377 YOUNG TED
298 STEMP GEORGE	338 WALLACE VIC(JNR)	
299 STEMP LES	339 WALLBANK ALAN	
300 STEVENS GEORGE	340 WALLER ALBERT	
301 STEWART(M-HURST)	341 WALTERS TONY	
302 STEWART BILL	342 WARD FRANK	
303 STOCKLEY ARTHUR(SNR)	343 WARD FRED	
304 STOCKLEY ARTHUR(JNR)	344 WARD JIM	
305 STOCKLEY LOU	345 WARREN JOHN	
306 STOKES BILL	346 WATKINS GEORGE	
307 STOUT TREVOR	347 WATSON GEORGE	
308 STRANGE CHARLIE	348 WEARN BERT	
309 SWEET BILL	349 WEBB HARRY	
310 TALBOT ROY	350 WEBB STAN	
311 TANN A	351 WEEKS REG	
312 TANNER BOB	352 WELCH BOB	
313 TAYLOR HAROLD	353 WELCH FRED	
314 TAYLOR ROLAND	354 WELCH LEN	
315 TAYLOR TOM	355 WEST FRED	
316 TERRY ROY	356 WESTON FRED	
317 THOMPSON GRAHAM	357 WHEELER REG	
318 TILL HAROLD	358 WHEELER ROGER	
319 TILL NIGEL	359 WHITCHER BRIAN	
320 TISDALL JOHN	360 WHITING DEREK	
321 TOMLIN DAVE	361 WICKERSON GEORGE	
322 TOOGOOD TONY	362 WIGHTMAN PAUL	
323 TOOLEY BOB	363 WILDS WILF	
324 TOSSELL PR (G-PORT)	364 WILKINS FRED	

RELIEF DRIVERS AND DRIVERS ASSISTANTS AT FRATTON TRAIN CREW DEPOT MAY 1984

BARTER MICK
BOYCE CHRIS
BROWN CHARLIE
BROWN GRAHAM
CANE ALAN
CORCORAN MARTIN
DAISH GARY
GORMAN ALAN
HASS
HURST DAVE
LEAVOLD BOB
PYMONT ALAN
SANKEY BOB
SILK BOB
SIMMONS DAVE
SIOU ANDY
THOMPSON GRAHAM
TOZER DAVE
WORBOYS KARL

Stan. Webb.
1999

115

CHAPTER 11

OFFICE AND SHED STAFF AS FROM 1942

MANAGEMENT	FITTERS (Cont'd)	COALMEN (Cont'd)	FRATTON LOCO CANTEEN
DOWNES STAN MPO	JONES TAFFY	HART TED	DAISH JOAN
EVERETT DICK	NEW RAY	HOLMES ALF	DURRANT MRS
NICHOLSON	RANCE JIM	HORN BILL	ELSTON MRS
FRY Miss	VANDRIES CHARLES	HOWE DICK	FOOT PEGGY
SMITH	WOODS JIM	JOLLIFFE CHARLIE	LOCKE CHARLIE (Nights)
BUTLER H *		LENTON TED	MAY
WRIGHT BERT		LOGAN JOCK	WALLACE BETTY
DENTON RAY	FITTERS AND BOILERSMITHS MATES	MARTIN ARTHUR	SHEILA
	BABS FRANK	SCARROT TED	
	BATCHELOR JOE	SCOWN TED (H-PORT)	
OFFICE STAFF	CHAMBERLAIN JUMBO	TIPPER COCK	
GASKIN NORMAN	DORRINGTON SHILO	TODD FRED	
JACKSON ERIC	HOLLAWAY RAY		LOCO'S AT FRATTON 1945
MARCHMENT LES	GRAINGER (Bills son)	FIREBARS BRICK-ARC	20, 27, 45, 54
SAXTON GWEN	KENNETT	VOKES DICK	114, 115, 118, 164, 166
SHARPE PAT	MCKAY ERNIE		172
SMITH GEORGE	NEWBIGGIN JOE		287, 300, 304, 338, 390
SMITH LES	STRANGE (Charlies son)	FOREMAN CLEANERS	400, 401, 417, 424, 425
TAYLOR GEORGE	WITTHIN BERT	BEECH ALF	441, 480
WHITE BERT			716, 756
WINDSOR ERIC			1796, 1797
WINDSOR TERRY	TURNTABLE MAINTENANCE	GENERAL LABOURERS	2139, 2260, 2269, 2490,
WRIGHT STAN	BAILEY PAT	CHAPMAN HARRY	2509, 2537, 2548, 255A,
		WILKINSON FRED	2549, 2562,
RUNNING FOREMEN	SHED DRAIN MAINTENANCE		2635, 2644, 2655, 2659,
BAKER CLARY	PHILLIPS GEORGE	ASH LOADER	2661, 2662, 2690, 2691,
BROWN PETE	AND COLLEAGUE	SMITH (ITCHY)	2694
DAVIS JIM			
DINGLEY PERCY			
DOWNES (SNR)	STORES ISSUERS	BREAKDOWN VANS GUARD	
HAND FRED	ANKERS ARTHUR	NEWMAN NOBBY	
HARRIS TED	SMITH SAM		
LUCKHAM TED	SOMERSET FRED	BREAKDOWN CRANE AT	
NEW TED	SPENCER ALF	HAVANT DURING WAR	
NEWPORT TOM	TURNER GEORGE	STURMEY JIM	
OLIVER ALF			
SMITH CHARLIE			
WARNER PAT	FIRELIGHTERS		
	BUNN JACK	RATCATCHER	
	COLLIS ALBIE	MIN (The cat)	
BOILERSMITH	HEATH FRED		
SMITH BERT	MARSH ALF		
FITTERS	COALCRANE DRIVERS		
ACKLAND BOB	BURTON SID		
BROWN JIM	COX ALF		
CLAYTON BILL	DAVIS		
COPE BILL	UPFIELD PAT		
GARNETT SID			
HAYES JACK	COALMEN		
HOOKWAY TONY	EDNEY PAT		

* FOREMAN

Perhaps the most unusual nickname applied to an animal at Fratton shed, this being Min the cat. Min, like its name, was thin but its role as "Rat catcher" kept the vermin away from the office area. This was a stray cat that became friendly, and was liked by the workers and staff. When free from its duties, Min would enjoy any food left-overs in the canteen area. The Rat catcher you could say, became one of the staff, so much so, that it appeared in Fratton depot's official STAFF LIST between t;he mid and late 1940s!

CHAPTER 12

MICHAEL HARVEY'S MEMORIES OF LOCAL STEAM

During the year of 1959 my note book captured no less than 72 "Hall" class and ten "Grange" class Western Region engines using the facilities at Fratton. WR "moguls" such as Nos. 6325, 7303 and 7324 were seen along with several "Manor" 4-6-0s, one of which was No. 7800 *Torquay Manor.*

London Midland "Black Five" 4-6-0s were also seen - but many more than we ever envisaged visited Portsmouth. Some of these, around 1963 were No. 44768 on a Sunday Excursion, No. 44770 with an Air Force troop train, No. 44909 (Excursion), No. 45046 on Saturdays Only train from Leeds and No. 45246 arriving at Fratton station (platform 2) at 5.30am employed on the overnight passenger/newspaper train from Waterloo.

Eastern Region steam were certainly the rarest visitors, and these consisted of class "B1" 4-6-0s on summer excursions to Portsmouth Harbour from the north London area. Noted were Nos. 61119 of Stratford depot (30A) on 6 May 1959 and 61200 of Kings Cross depot (34A) in July 1961, no doubt, there were others during this period. One special mention dated September 1966 saw No. 60103 pass through Cosham with a London (Victoria) to Eastleigh Special excursion hauled by that Eastern Region's famous *Flying Scotsman* via Haywards Heath, Hove, Havant, Fareham and Botley in September 1966. No. 60103 being, at that date, preserved.

"Britannia" class steam did come both into Fratton depot and also along the top of Cosham triangle. These "pacifics" only built in 1951, had a very short life-span. Those recorded were Nos. 70000 *Britannia,* 70002 *Geoffrey Chaucer,* 70004 *William Shakespeare,* 70017 *Arrow,* 70019 *Lightning,* 70037 *Hereward the Wake* and 70047.

Being on the Southern Region, Fratton obviously had numerous SR steam classes using the depot facilities, but there were always some unusual types, such as class "D1" 4-4-0 no. 31735, class "L1" 4-4-0 No. 31757 (stored), class "P" 0-6-0 tank No. 31556 (now preserved on the Bluebell Steam Railway) and class "A1" 0-6-0 tanks Nos. DS680 and DS681.

A November 1959 list of locomotives "on shed" as seen by Michael:

FRATTON DEPOT

30022	30039	30328	30357
30496	30545	30726	30729
30732	30856	31408	31637
31807	31809	31895	32139
32337	32349	32479	32495
32509	32548	32549	32640
32650	32661	32677	32694
76017	76059		

Of the 30 noted, 20 were allocated to Fratton.

Unusual freight steam locomotives were very few and far between but I did observe a class "WD" 2-8-0 No. 90261 of Feltham depot (70B) and formerly of Banbury (84D), employed on the 12.15pm passenger train to Plymouth (as far as Fareham) this being in August 1960.

A class "8F" 2-8-0 No. 48408 was noted passing through Cosham with a freight from the south Wales area in 1960, again, further "8F" engines used the north side of the Cosham triangle.

MICHAEL HARVEY HAS OVER THE YEARS, ACCUMULATED NUMEROUS CLASSES OF LOCOMOTIVES.

THIS LIST BEING TAKEN FROM HIS LOCAL TRAVELS OF JUNE AND JULY 1963:

Use of several "Run-about" tickets gave me the chance to visit some locations such as Bognor, Hayling Island, Winchester and Chichester.

SAT. 8 JUNE: Fareham, Class "9F" 2-10-0 No 92239 en route to Fratton

SAT. 20 JUNE: Cosham. "West Country" 4-6-2 No. 34014 "Budleigh Salterton" with Brighton to Exeter passenger train.

SAT. 20 JUNE: Hayling Island. "A1X" 0-6-0s Nos. 32650 and 32670.

MON. 22 JULY: Chichester. "Q1" 0-6-0 No. 33031 shunting duties, near former Midhurst branch area.

SUN. 1 JULY: Bognor, Class "4" 2-6-0 Standard No. 76064 in station sidings. Out of use. Probably awaiting to being assisted to either Fratton or Eastleigh.

MON. 29 JULY: Southampton. Standard class "4" 2-6-0 No. 76009 hauling the 12.15pm Portsmouth and Southsea to Plymouth working via Salisbury.

MON. 29 JULY: HILSEA. Class. "Q" 0-6-0 No. 30543 employed on the Bertram Mills Circus train. Then following it to Fratton station where it reversed into Fyffes Banana siding, where several elephants were led through the streets of Southsea to Southsea Common, this was where the circus was being set up.

SUN. 21 JULY Fratton. Midland Region 2-6-2 Ivatt tank No, 41325, and "S15" 4-6-0 No. 30838.

NOTE: THERE MUST HAVE BEEN NUMEROUS OTHER SIGHTINGS OF THOSE CLASSES ABOVE ALSO OTHER CLASSES THAT WENT UNSEEN.

Wainwright SECR class "P" 0-6-0 tank No. 31556, it was designed for push-and-pull working. Introduced in 1909. Loaned to Fratton from Brighton depot (75A) to replace an "A1X" on the Hayling branch that had gone to Eastleigh Works 1960 - it was not required.   *John Spence*

CHAPTER 13

THE LAST STEAM LOCOMOTIVE OUT OF FRATTON

Going back to chapter one of this book we read about how the very first steam train into Portsmouth proved rather embarrassing for the railway company - this being on 14 June 1847. The ensuing 120 years up until the LAST steam locomotive departed in July 1967 the observers of the iron horse in the Portsmouth area were blessed with its numerous steam workings and tremendous variety of railway locomotive types. The drivers and firemen enjoyed the job that they were proud of, and getting paid for their efforts, even though their working conditions resulted in being covered in coal dust and sweat - it was their work, and brought an income for their families.

Sunday 9 July, 1967 was indeed a sad day, not only for the Fratton railwaymen but also for those local railway enthusiasts as the final engine steamed out of Fratton yard - it would be another 28 years before another was to be seen!

It was originally thought that Standard class "5" 4-6-0 No. 73029 in green livery (under the grime) was to be the final steam locomotive - and this appeared to be the case.

The final departure from Fratton sidings on that Sunday morning, was indeed No. 73029. As it slowly pulled out of the Field sidings with a long rake of empty carriages bound for Clapham Junction sidings - the whistle was constantly blowing off! The smoke box door exclaimed "PLAY UP POMPEY" chalked in large capital letters.

It was learned at a later date, that when a steam locomotive was performing its final duty, prior to withdrawal, its crew would be constantly sounding its whistle for the duration of its journey!

But, as it transpired, later that afternoon, the Guildford depot "pilot" No. 30072, a class "USA" 0-6-0 tank, was also making its final journey out of the semi round house bound for Salisbury depot yard, where it would be in the company of 60 or so other steam locomotives, all which were awaiting their turn to be towed to the scrap yards in South Wales.

On reaching Havant, having ran "light" via Petersfield and Rowlands Castle, it was realised that the small side tanks of the "USA" needed replenishing and it also needed more coal to enable it to reach Salisbury. After contact with Fratton depot staff, the driver of No. 30072, was informed to take the line into Portsmouth and to take on its requirements at Fratton depot. So, as it worked out - the "USA" was the FINAL steam engine to leave BOTH Guildford AND Fratton sheds!

To add a little history, as far as it is known, this was the FIRST time that a class "USA" 0-6-0 tank had visited Fratton. It took its quota of coal from the steam crane DS200, which "Jumbo" Collis was the operator, he had assumed that the Standard class"5" 4-6-0 was his last duty, but indeed, it was not. Luckily, No. 30072 was rescued from the "dead" lines at Salisbury depot yard after laying there for several months. It was purchased by officials from the Keighley and Worth Valley preserved railway located in North Yorkshire - it was eventually restored to running use, and can still he seen at the Keighley and Worth Valley Railway - AND THE STORY HAD A HAPPY ENDING!

Left and above: The Goldsmith Avenue main entrance to Fratton locomotive depot had these warning signs clearly displayed, but I and other train-spotters repeatedly ignored these, and we were constantly "nabbed" by the foreman. It is ironic that these signs were virtually the last to be removed from this area in the late 1960s. *Both photographs by Steve Hayward.*

No. 30072 was the last-steam locomotive to depart from Fratton depot on Sunday 9 July 1967.

CHAPTER 14

ERIC: A TRAVELLING RAILWAY PHOTOGRAPHER

IF YOU EVER HAD ANY THOUGHTS THAT ERIC RESTRICTED HIS RAILWAY PICTURES ONLY TO THE PORTSMOUTH AREA, THEN THINK AGAIN ... HE ALSO TRAVELLED TO MANY OTHER LOCATIONS.

Eric, with his trusty Pentax camera found time during the early 1960s to photograph steam on the BR system. He frequently made visits from his home city of Portsmouth to such locations as the Midlands, Crewe, the North West, London and even as far north as Carlisle - and other locations, a little nearer, such as Basingstoke. The following selection of Eric's photographic gems will give you proof of his forays up and down the country in search of steam. Unfortunately, he did not provide all locations for these pictures, but drawing on my knowledge of railways, I have included some brief captions.

Class "5" (Black Five) 4-6-0 No. 45414 with a 8B shed-plate' Edge Hill (Liverpool).

"Princess Coronation" class 4-6-2 No. 46255 *City of Hereford*. Introduced in 1938 for main-line working. Allocated to Carlisle (Kingsmoor) depot 12A.

Three locomotives at Uttoxeter (shed code 5F). Only the two on the right are known, they are class "4MT" 2-6-4 tank No. 42670 and class "3F" 0-6-0 tank No. 47606 - a "Jinty" tank.

No. 43284 is quite an ancient locomotive, it is a class "3F" 0-6-0 introduced in 1885. It was a Johnson Midland rebuild.

A Crewe North (5A) allocation. "Princess Coronation" class 4-6-2 No. 46235 *City of Birmingham*. Now in static preservation.

Reading General is the location of this "Castle" class 4-6-0 No. 7021 *Haverfordwest Castle* as it awaits signals for its departure to London (Paddington). Note: the reporting code 724 above smoke box door, this train being the 7.05 am from Cheltenham.

This is a "Merchant Navy" class locomotive entering the "up" platforms at Basingstoke station, it is employed on a Weymouth to London (Waterloo) express. The engine is No. 35018 *British India Line* and, today it is in the stages of preservation at Carnforth, Lancashire. On the right is part of Basingstoke depot (70D), now long demolished. Summer 1960.

Class "4900" (Hall) 4-6-0 No. 6936 *Breccles Hall*. It spent most of its life allocated to depots in South Wales and the West of England.

Gresley designed class "A4" 4-6-2 No. 60003 *Andrew K. McCosh*. London, Kings Cross (34A) allocation. Built at Doncaster in 1937.

An Ivatt rebuild of a Fowler design "Patriot" class, No. 45512 *Bunsen*. Introduced 1946. Shed plate is 12F, a Workington allocation.

Class "2P" 4-4-0 No. 40404 Introduced in 1912. Note: tank (on left) and possible engine shed (right).

Basingstoke is the location of this marvellous picture of "West Country" class 4-6-2 No. 34099 *Lynmouth* hurrying through the station with a northbound passenger train for London (Waterloo). Note part of the engine shed (70D) - on the far right.

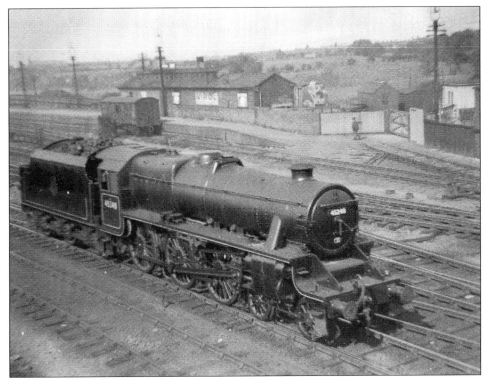

The background to this picture could be used in a model railway layout, as there are many objects that make an ideal scene. The locomotive is an ex-works condition "Black Five" 4-6-0 No. 45248.

Grimy and work-stained fits the description of this un-identified class "8F" 2-8-0 lurking in a roundhouse that has seen better days! Location could be the Birmingham based depot of Saltley (21A).

Eastern Region class "A2" 4-6-2 No. 60522 *Straight Deal* letting off some steam. Locomotives of this class carried names taken from race horses of the 1930s. This is a Thompson design, Introduced In 1944. Note the shed plate (50A) York depot - and the letters "SC" which tells you that it had a Self-Cleaning smoke box. Mostly used to haul passenger trains between London (Kings Cross) to Edinburgh and beyond via the East Coast main line.

The train engine is a Standard class "5" 4-6-0 No. 73016 being assisted by a class "4P" (Compound) 4-4-0. No. 41050 employed on a passenger working.

Absolutely spotless condition class "5" (Black Five) 4-6-0 No. 45295. It is displaying a 12B shed plate - a Carlisle (Upperby) allocation. Note: the massive coaling plant in the background. Locations for this page were not provided.

Western Region class "6800" (Grange) 4-6-0 No. 6871 *Bourton Grange*, photographed from the station platform at Basingstoke. The depot is in the background. A late 1950s picture.

Eric Grace and some of his workers from Fratton depot frequented this area, near the Battledown flyover, just a few miles south of Basingstoke to capture pictures. This May 1963 picture shows Standard class "5" 4-6-0 No. 73118 hauling a Waterloo to west of England train.

A Beyer-Garratt 2-6-6-2 wheel arrangement. This is No. 47985, introduced in 1927. It is a Fowler and Beyer-Peacock design. An early 1950s picture.

Class "A4" 4-6-2 No. 60022 *Mallard* employed on "The Elizabethan" working between London (Kings Cross) and Edinburgh (Waverley). This locomotive holds the World speed record for a steam locomotive of 126mph in 1937.

Class "WD" 2-8-0 heavy freight locomotive No. 90268 - it is in a very grimy condition. as were most heavy freight types.

Marvellous station scene! A "Black Five" 4-6-0 No. 45277 awaits its departure. Its depot of allocation, from its shed-plate (6G) is Llandudno Junction. Locations for the pictures on this page were not provided.

We are now "overseas" - but its only the Isle of Wight! This scene shows two class "O2" 0-4-4 tanks at Ryde depot (70H) in 1963. No. 29 is named *Alverstone*.

This was one of only four class "5" (Black Five) 4-6-0s that carried nameplates during the British Railways days. There were no less than 842 of these built to a William Stanier design. The name of this locomotive was *Ayrshire Yeomanry* - and it was numbered 45156.

Class "Princess Coronation" 4-6-2 No. 46244 *King George VI*. Location, for the picture on this page was not provided.

Eric Grace and Jeff Wyncoll both visited Basingstoke and area to capture steam in action. Here we see Standard class "5" 4-6-0 near the Battledown flyover.

This idyllic background forms the setting for an LMS class "4P" (Compound) 4-4-0 No. 41120, this three cylinder locomotive was introduced in 1924. Location for this picture was not provided.

A Western Region class "1000" (County) 4-6-0 No. 1021 *County of Montgomery*. This class consisted of 30 engines and they were built to a Hawkesworth design in 1945. Its allocation, in the early 1950s was Penzance (83G).

Churchward designed class "2800" 2-8-0 heavy freight locomotive No. 2824. Possible location being a South Wales depot. A mid 1950s picture. Locations for the pictures on this page were not provided.

With its number obliterated, this class "2P 2-4-2 tank awaits its fate at possibly Uttoxeter depot (5F). Note the tarpaulin over its chimney. Mid 1950s.

At the capital - a diesel hydraulic slowly makes its way into Paddington station. A mid 1960s picture.

Class "MN" (Merchant Navy) 4-6-2 No. 35027 *Port Line* awaits its departure from London (Victoria) station with the "Golden Arrow" express to Dover. Note the railwaymen on the track - no high-visible clothing in those days! Also note the No. "4" duty on the right-hand white disc. and the close proximity of the houses backing onto the railway. Date of photograph is summer 1958.

The same locomotive and train, showing the well filled tender of coal. Both the driver and fireman are eagerly awaiting the "right away" from Victoria station.

Eastern Region class "A3" 4-6-2 No. 60097 *Humorist*. Introduced 1927. Fitted with Kylchap blast pipe and double chimney. A 1960 picture - at that date it was allocated to Haymarket depot (64B) Edinburgh.

"Britannia" class 4-6-2 No. 70004 *William Shakespeare*. En route between London and Dover.

An early 1960s picture. Around this date No. 70004 had classmate No. 70014 *Iron Duke* allocated to Stewarts Lane depot (73A) primarily to work the prestigious "GOLDEN ARROW" express from London (Victoria) to Dover.

Above: Class "LN" (Lord Nelson) 4-6-0 No. 30850 *Lord Nelson*. Eastleigh depot (71A). Early 1960s.

Below: Class "A4" 4-6-2 No. 60034 *Lord Faringdon*. Fitted with Kylchap blast pipe and double chimney.

A CLASS "LI" EASTERN REGION STEAM LOCOMOTIVE

This Eastern Region class "LI" 2-6-4 tank No. 67790 was one of a 100 of this class introduced between 1945 and 1954 to a Thompson design. It was allocated to Neasden (34E) in the north west area of London in the mid 1950s - which gives a clue of this pictures' location.

London Midland Region class "8P" main-line pacific No. 46220 *Coronation* is running "light" near Willesden depot (1A). This is a William Stanier design introduced in 1938. Originally streamlined. Photograph taken in the mid 1950s, at that date Coronation was allocated to Polmadie (Glasgow), code 66A.

One of a class of 30 "MN" (Merchant Navy) 4-6-2s designed by Oliver Bulleid and introduced in 1941, No. 35008 *Orient Line*, is seen here, rebuilt without its original streamline casing employed on a Weymouth to London (Waterloo) passenger train in the early 1960s. This location, near Basingstoke, was one of Eric's favourite photographic spots, usually when accompanied by Jeff Wyncoll, as mentioned in previous pages.

Eastleigh depot (71A), later down-graded to 70E prior to its closure in July, 1967, was Eric's very first workplace before he joined his home city depot of Fratton. This picture sees a Bulleid "pacific" lurking behind a class "U1" 2-6-0 No. 31898 - this "mogul" was designed by Maunsell and introduced in 1928. No. 31898 was allocated to Stewarts Lane (73A) - note its connecting rods have been removed, it is waiting to be towed by a class "33" diesel to a South Wales scrap yard via Salisbury - picture taken July 1963.

The driver of class "4900" (Hall) class 4-6-0 No. 4934 *Hindlip Hall* is looking a bit concerned over a leak. It is thought that this picture was taken at Reading (General) station and the locomotive was employed on a West of England to London (Paddington) train, as its allocation was 83A Newton Abbot. Note the old style porters trolley on the platform (left). A late 1950s picture.

No guesses for the location of this picture - it is the familiar background of Swindon Locomotive Works and the newly out-shopped class "4900" (Hall) 4-6-0 No. 6958 *Oxburgh Hall*. It has not yet been re-united with its tender, this was the usual procedure whenever an engine with a tender had been overhauled. A mid 1950s picture.

No location provided for this excellent shot of London Midland Region class "7P" (Royal Scot) 4-6-0 No. 46116, *Irish Guardsman*. Introduced 1941. A William Stanier rebuild of a Fowler design that was introduced in 1927. Allocation of this engine was Carlisle (Upperby) (12A).

Typical Western Region engine shed yard view with "Castle" class 4-6-0 No. 7037 *Swindon* awaiting its next duty. Collett design introduced 1946 - aptly named Swindon, as it was the final "Castle" class locomotive built at Swindon Works. Possible location of this picture could be Southall (81C).

No location of this Eric Grace picture, but its details and history need some explanation. No. 46100 *Royal Scot* is a class "7P" 4-6-0 locomotive designed by William Stanier - it is a rebuild of a Fowler locomotive that was introduced in 1927. Its work consisted mainly of passenger trains between London (Euston) and Scotland, Glasgow (Central) together with other main line duties. Allocation was Camden depot (1B) during the late 1950s, and I recall noting it quite often whilst on train-spotting trips to London. No. 46100 had the distinction of being shipped over to America in 1933 (at that date it was numbered 6100 and on its arrival was given a commemorative bell displayed on its buffer beam).

The lettering displayed below its nameplate gives the following details:

This locomotive with the Royal Scot train was exhibited at the century of progress exposition, Chicago 1933 and made a tour of the Dominion of Canada and the United States of America. The engine and train covered 11,194 miles over the railroads of the north American continent and was inspected by 3,021,601 people.

R. Gilbertson - Driver   **T. Blackett - Fireman**
J. Jackson - Fireman   **W. C. Woods - Fitter**

BASINGSTOKE STATION:
Class "Hall" 4-6-0 No. 6915 *Mursley Hall* making its way south with an excursion from the Chester area, its destination was probably Portsmouth or Bournemouth. It carries a Reporting code above its front number plate "030". Summer 1961.

Drummond design class "T9" 4-4-0 No. 30287 an Eastleigh allocated engine on its home patch. Note the clean condition of this passenger locomotive and the familiar black and white corrugated structure which made pictures taken at Eastleigh easily recognisable. Used mainly on the Portsmouth to Southampton Central passenger services. Built 1899 and withdrawn late 1950s. A 1957 picture.

This is the sole class "T9" 4-4-0 to be taken into preservation - numbered 30120, and then returned to No. 120 in which form it is seen here and pictured inside Eastleigh depots' 16 lane straight shed. It has had spells on various preserved railways, and is at present at the Bluebell Steam Railway.

No. 5050 AGAIN - BUT NOT AT FRATTON . . .

Eric Grace took this photograph but gave no indication of its location, and from the background, it might be taken as Swindon. It was obviously prior to its "impounding" at Fratton during the summer of 1963 - the locomotive being "Castle" class 4-6-0 No : 5050 *Earl of St. Germans*. Probably an early 1960s picture.

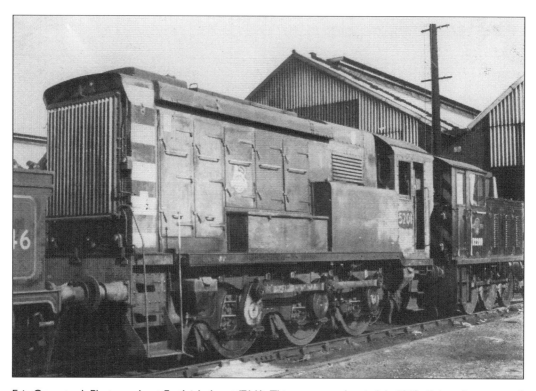

Eric Grace took Photographs at Eastleigh depot (71A). This one was taken in July 1963. Being a "steam man" he rarely captured diesel pictures but, by this date, they were well into the scene. The picture shows an 0-6-0 diesel electric shunting locomotive No. 15201 it was introduced in 1937. Behind is a small diesel mechanical 0-6-0 No. D2252. This type used at Southampton Docks for light shunting work

The early 1960s saw the withdrawal of many British Railways steam locomotives. New types of motive power, such as diesel electrics were taking over the steam duties. Main line locomotives like No. 10000 (below) were in fact, built as early as 1947 and were possibly the fore-runners of the class "37s" that were to be introduced many years later.

Is this the shape of things to come? Not too many of this type of motive power was snapped with the Pentax camera! The diesel electric locomotive is No. 10000 6P/5F "Co-Co", introduced in 1947. It was an English Electric Co and H. G. Ivatt design primarily for working main-line passenger trains on the LMSR route between London (Euston) and Glasgow (Central). No. 10001 was photographed at Euston in the late 1950s.

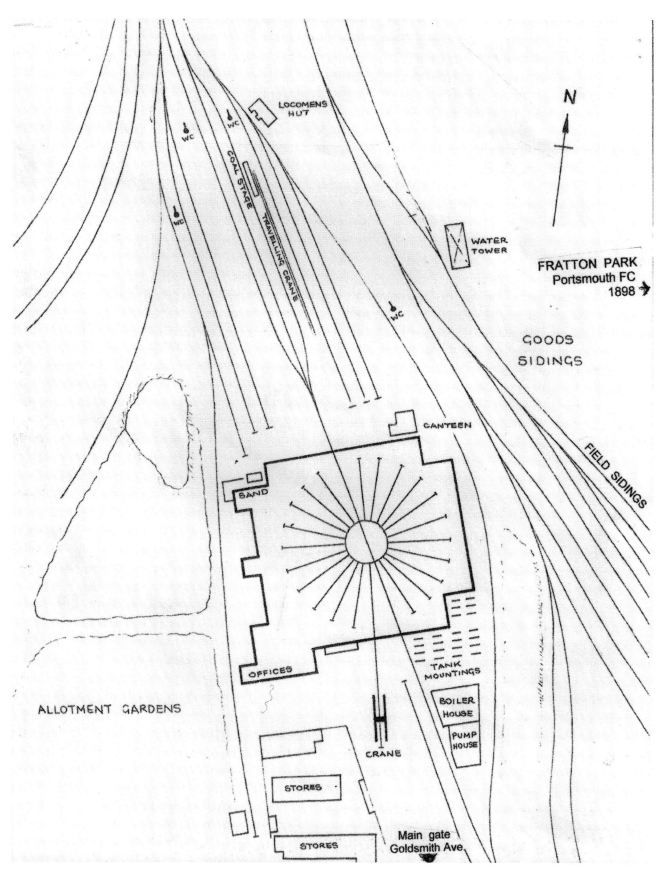

Detailed layout of Fratton Locomotive Depot, showing the 50 foot turn-table, tracks and siding in the yard, water tower and extensive goods sidings, amongst other points of interest. The depot was built in 1891. A mid 1950s plan.

Hand drawing by kind permission of Graham Beech.

FRATTON: TWO MAIN-LINE LOCOMOTIVES PENDING PRESERVATION, AND A NAME-PLATE GOES MISSING . . .

Having been shunted out of the roundhouse where they were under cover and reasonably safe, class "LN" 4-6-0 No. 30850 *Lord Nelson* and class "N15" 4-6-0 No. 30777 *Sir Lamiel*, find themselves in the yard in the mid 1960s awaiting their turn to be towed away for preservation. These two have since been returned to main-line working order. The group of class "U" 2-6-0s and class "4" Standards (right) were not so lucky, they, at a later date, went to the breaker's yards. A train-spotting colleague of mine (whose name will remain anonymous) claims to have removed one of the name-plates from No. 30777 soon after it was put into the roundhouse, and the railway police were attempting to locate its whereabouts. When my colleague got news of this, he was claimed to have got a "bit hot under the collar" and disposed of it in the nearby entrance of the canal at Milton - these remarks are obviously un-confirmed - who knows - it might still be there today.

Steam crane DS200 forms the focal point of this typical view.

ONE OF ERIC GRACE'S FAVOURITE ENGINES

STEAM LOCOMOTIVES ALLOCATED TO FRATTON DEPOT (70F) - WINTER 1955-1956

Class "M7" 0-4-4 tanks Nos. 30022 and 30039.

Class "02" 0-4-4 tank No. 30207.

Class "T9" 4-4-0s Nos. 30337, 30726, 30729, 30730, 30732.

Class "U" 2-6-0s Nos. 31612, 31637, 31638. 31805, 31807, 31808 and 31809.

Class "K" 2-6-0s Nos. 32337 and 32349.

Class "E4" 0-6-2 tanks Nos. 32479, 32495, 32505 and 32509.

Class "C2X" 0-6-0s Nos. 32548, 32549 and 32550.

Class "E1" 0-6-0 tanks Nos. 32138, 32139 and 32694.

Class "A1X" 0-6-0 tanks Nos. 32650, 32661 and 32677.   TOTAL = 30

ONE OF THE LAST GWR "HALL" CLASS TO VISIT PORTSMOUTH

Class "4900" (Hall) 4-6-0, N. 6953 *Leighton Hall*. A summer 1965 photograph. Its shed plate and name plates have been removed. By this date, many Western Region steam locomotives had been withdrawn. All GWR workings ceased on 31 December 1965.

THANK YOU FOR YOUR CONTRIBUTIONS

John Barrowdale; Basil Batten (the late); Graham Beech; George Blakey; H. C. Casserley; Alf Coffin (the late); Colin Cromwell; Tom H. Dethridge; Ann Grace; Ann Harvey; Sandy Hayward; Steve Hayward; George Lee; Ernie Middleton (the late); Brain Moss; Dave Pallett; Colin Robins; Eddie Rooke; Colin Saunders; John Scutt; Fred Somerset (the late); John Spence; Derek Spicer; N. E. Stead; Len Worboys; Phil Ward; Stan Webb and Doug Willis. Please accept my sincere apologies if I have omitted anyone.

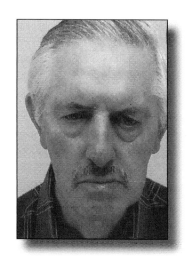

ABOUT THE AUTHOR

Readers of Michael's four published books, mostly relating to train-spotting, will know that he spent much of the period from the mid 1950s up to when Standard gauge steam finished in August 1968 travelling around England, Scotland and Wales to see as much of the steam scene as was financially possible, with annual leave permitting.

Rarely a weekend went by without him going somewhere, but this did not prevent him watching many local goings on in his home city of Portsmouth.

This would find him either on Fratton station footbridge or at a vantage point from Goldsmith Avenue to observe the passing trains and the many "light" engine movements. If he was not there he would be "bunking" the local Fratton engine shed!

Visiting this shed scene area, Michael had witnessed the sights captured so well by the photography displayed in this book emanating from the camera of the late Eric Grace.

His fondness for the environs of the Fratton railway area come through in the script of this book, and his interesting detailed photo captions. I have only known Michael for the last 25 years, but he has a good memory of steam events and many unusual steam workings into Portsmouth during the first 19 years of British Railways Nationalisation.

His interest in the city of his birth goes beyond railways as he has a good knowledge of its local ships, buses, pop music scene, cinemas, dance halls and industry – and of course, his beloved Portsmouth Football Club "Pompey" which he supported both home and away between 1949 and 2009.

I hope that you get as much enjoyment reading this book as Michael did compiling it.

John Borrowdale

Many thanks for the help of Carrol Reed, Gail Baird and Bob Hind for their knowledge and effort during the latter stages of the book, it is very much appreciated.

CLASS 'Z' 0-8-0 TANK No. 30951

STANDARD '3" 2-6-2 TANK No. 82012

"BLACK FIVE" 4-6-0

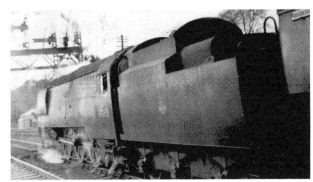

CLASS 'BB' 4-6-2 No. 34065 *Hurricane*

"N15" 4-6-0 No. 30785 *Sir Mador de la Porte*

CLASS "3" 0-6-0 TANK No. 47338

CLASS '4300' 2-6-0 No. 6312

CLASS "O2" 0-4-4 TANK No. 30177

"BLACK FIVE" 4-6-0

"CASTLE" 4-6-0 No. 5068 *Beverston Castle*

TODAY: Fratton locomotive depot, its roundhouse, yards, buildings and huts and the massive goods depot have all been obliterated from the scene; replaced by new road systems, leading to Fratton Park, a massive hotel, a McDonalds and the largest B&Q warehouse in Europe! It was from reliable sources, that when the final steam engine left the depot yard in July 1967, railwaymen deposited many of their tools in the six feet deep inspection pits along with their shovels and other items such as "Not to be moved" signs, shed plates and grease top caps! Perhaps in future years, if any excavation for additional construction takes place, a treasure trove might come to light?

THE END

My special thanks to Ann Grace for her kind permission to allow the publishing of the late Eric Grace photographs.

If you have enjoyed reading this book and would like to come along to some of the local railway and transport societies monthly meetings, you and your guests would be most welcome. You do not need to belong to the clubs' venue - all they ask is a small donation to help keep the club running. Name of club and telephone are briefly as follows: Portsmouth Regional Group of the Mid Hants Railway Preservation Society 02392-671-251. Meon Valley Locomotive Society 01489-894-051. Portsmouth Vintage Transport Group 02392-738-768. The Railway Correspondence and Travel Society 01794-390-241. Gosport Railway Society 02392-523-238. Southern Counties Railway Society 02380-293-186. The Sandown Railway Enthusiasts Society 01983-405-60. MHRPS/RCTS 02380-849-533. The Stan Micklewright Railway Club 01962-866-89. The Ffestiniog Railway Club 01329-667-315. NOTE: telephone numbers change quite often, as their secretaries leave resulting in another committee member taking over. M. G. Harvey.